Hidden Florida Keys and Everglades

The Adventurer's Guide

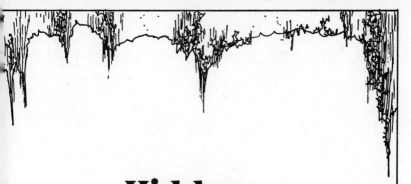

Hidden
Florida Keys
and
Everglades

The Adventurer's Guide

Candace Leslie

Executive Editor   Ray Riegert

ULYSSES PRESS

To Bob,
Who always encourages

Published by: Ulysses Press
Sather Gate Station
Box 4000–H
Berkeley, CA 94704

Library of Congress Catalog Card Number 89-051439
ISBN   0 915233 19 3

Printed in the U.S.A. by the George Banta Company

10 9 8 7 6 5 4 3 2

Production Director: Leslie Henriques
Managing Editor: Lindsay Mugglestone
Editor: Judith Kahn
Editorial Associate: Claire Chun

Illustrator: Norman Nicholson
Cartographer: Robert Lettieri
Cover Designers: Leslie Henriques and Phil Gardner
Indexer: Sayre Van Young

Cover Photography: Front cover by Dave Houser; back cover by Cliff Hollenbeck and Ed Simpson

Published in the United Kingdom and Europe by:
Moorland Publishing Company, Ltd.
Moor Farm Road West
Ashbourne, England, DE6 1HD
UK ISBN 0 86190 359 5

Notes from the Publisher

* * *

Throughout the text, hidden locales, remote regions, and little-known spots are marked with a star (★).

* * *

An alert, adventurous reader is as important as a travel writer in keeping a guidebook up-to-date and accurate. So if you happen upon a great restaurant, discover a hidden locale, or (heaven forbid) find an error in the text, we'd appreciate hearing from you. Just write to:

Ulysses Press
Box 4000–H
Berkeley, CA 94704

* * *

It is our desire as publishers to create guidebooks that are responsible as well as informative. The danger of exploring hidden locales is that they will no longer be secluded.

We hope that our guidebooks treat the people, country and land we visit with respect. We ask that our readers do the same. The hiker's motto, "Walk softly on the Earth," applies to travelers everywhere . . . in the desert, on the beach, and in town.

* * *

CONTENTS

SPECIAL FEATURES

MAPS

ONE

Keys and Everglades Dreaming

The Why, When and How
of Traveling in the Florida Keys and Everglades

Why

The Everglades. The Keys. There are no places like them anywhere on earth. The one is mysterious. The other romantic. Though neighbors, they are alike mainly in their uniqueness. Prominent on maps, they are fragile on the earth, homes to endangered species, dependent on the diligence of humankind for their very survival. For the traveler, they are exotic worlds at the tip of a colorful state long famous for its ability to beckon sojourners and settlers. As tourist destinations, they were late on the bandwagon, partly because of their distance from the rest of the nation and partly because nature kept them inaccessible for so long. But they have now emerged as South Florida's two greatest treasures.

The Everglades, a great, broad and shallow, life-giving river, long kept its secrets to itself in the dark reaches of cypress swamp and deep, watery grasses. In fact, much of the vast wetlands is still inaccessible, and some of the more remote hammocks and islets remain unexplored. But not all. Today the traveler can easily enter portions of this subtle, curious, jungly world, thanks to skillfully designed roads and paths provided by the planners and developers of the Everglades National Park. Today you can venture through once-impenetrable hardwood hammocks, walk safely among alligators, count endangered wood storks on a tree branch, discover brilliant snails on fragile plant stems, stoop down and observe clear, quiet water ceaselessly flowing through tall sawgrass, watch waterfowl winging their way home, silhouetted against a brilliant sunset sky.

1

Animals and plants from both temperate and tropical zones inhabit this crossover environment. For those searching for hidden destinations, the Everglades is a treasure trove. Even a short walk will introduce you to a host of secrets and likely inspire you to probe ever more deeply. Whether on foot or paddling a canoe, you can follow any of a host of well-designed trails that beckon you into the heart and soul of the subtropics. The longer you stay and the deeper you explore, the greater will be your rewards.

The same can be said of a journey to the Keys, which appear like a sprinkling of afterthought on the tip of the Florida map. In reality, they are a chain of lush subtropical islands built on ancient coral reefs, floating like an emerald necklace that marks the meeting of the Atlantic Ocean and the Gulf of Mexico. Their history resounds with tales of pirate treasure and fortunes gleaned from ships tossed to bits on the still-living reefs that lie a few miles to the east out in the ocean. Long accessible only by boat, today 36 jewels of this necklace are joined by the great Overseas Highway. Fishing craft have replaced the pirate ships; scuba divers and snorkelers now explore the reefs where ships once met their dooms. Artists, adventurers and other free spirits call these isles home.

To the south and east of the Keys lies the Atlantic Ocean, usually as calm as a lake, held in check by the coral reef. On the other side, broad, shallow Florida Bay bounds the Upper Keys, opening into the Gulf of Mexico as the islands curve out beyond the tip of the state. Except in stormy weather, these waters to the north and west of the islands also lap the shore with a gentle touch. This lack of wave action means there are very few sandy beaches in the Keys, but water on both sides of the islands rivals the Caribbean in its clarity and its brilliant greens and blues.

Just driving down the Keys can be a thrill. There's something exciting about being able to view the sea on all sides from a bridge seven miles long, about finding tropical trees that grow nowhere else in the country, about visiting a house built in the Bahamas and delivered to Key West on a sailing ship. But with the thrill also comes a subtle slowing down, as if the farther out to sea you go, the less the clock matters. Keys folks are proud of this casual, laid-back lifestyle that is impossible to ignore. The best thing you can do is enter into its relaxing spirit by discarding your watch and letting the sun and sea rule your days and the moon and stars your nights. And, remember, surprises are here for the finding. If you look beyond the billboards, down side streets, over on the neighboring out-islands or under the sea, you'll be rewarded with plenty of hidden sights.

This book is designed to help you explore these very differing regions of South Florida. It takes you to countless popular spots and offers advice on how best to enjoy them. It leads you into some off-the-beaten-path locales, places you learn about by talking with folks at the neighborhood fish market or with someone who has lived in the area all his life. It acquaints you with the area's history, its natural habitats and its residents, both human and animal. It recommends sights that should not be missed. It suggests places to eat, to lodge, to play, to camp, always with consideration for varying interests, budgets and tastes.

The traveling part of this book begins with the Everglades, presenting in Chapter Two the main visitor accesses to this wild natural region as explored via the three entrances to the national park. Included in this chapter, too, are nearby destinations, both natural and manmade. Chapter Three heads down the Florida Keys, "the islands you can drive to," through Key Largo, Islamorada and Marathon, all the way to Big Pine and the Lower

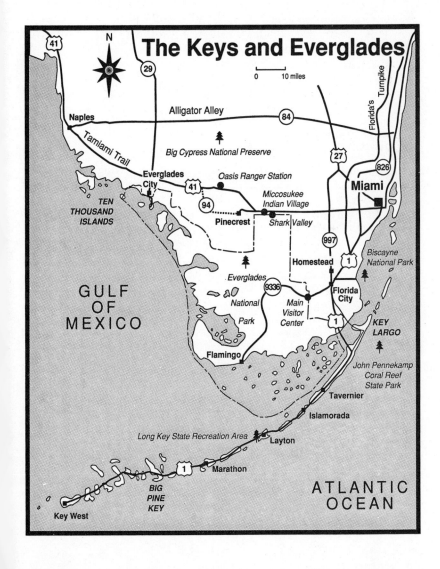

Keys. History and hype merge in Chapter Four, a guide to Key West, famous party town, arts center and ethnic village, whose romantic past and charm still color its life.

Where you go and what you choose to see is up to you—these areas include enough sights and activities to appeal to a very broad range of interests. This is verified by the numbers of retired people who return annually or settle down here, by the families who arrive each summer as soon as school is out, by the folks who come in their boats and tie up for a stay, as well by as the fanciers of the fast lane who come to live it up in Key West. For lovers of birds and wildlife and quiet, breathtaking beauty, there are few places as rewarding as the Everglades. For those who fish and dive or simply love the sea, the Keys offer all you could wish for.

These are southern Florida's two great gems. May they hold for you all kinds of hidden, and even not-so-hidden, rewards.

The Story of the Keys and Everglades

GEOLOGY

As land masses go, all of Florida is a mere child, having emerged from the sea as recently as 20 to 30 million years ago. For eons its bedrock base lay beneath the warm waters of the southern sea. Slowly it collected sediment, building limestone deposits that would eventually rise above the surface. As distant glaciers froze and melted, the seas rose and fell, forming and reforming the shores of Florida, depositing silt and bits of sea life.

The Everglades actually begin at Lake Okeechobee, and to learn their geology, one must look to this shallow lake whose rocky foundation lies only a few feet above sea level. Beneath the lake and extending down into the northern part of the Everglades, the rock is a limestone composed of alternating layers of hardened sea bottom and of freshwater peats and muds. Farther south, it becomes a more porous limestone known as oolite. The surface of this spongy layer often becomes full of holes that have been receptacles for decaying vegetation, fresh water, sand and shells.

Beneath these relatively "young" limestone formations lies the oldest rock in southern Florida, the impervious *Tamiami* formation. Like a giant underground cistern, it collects and holds the rainwater that falls on the spongy Everglades limestones and on Big Cypress Swamp. Surrounding cities such as Miami and Palm Beach, as well as the Florida Keys, depend on this life-giving reservoir for their survival. The force and power of this giant aquifer also keep the seawater at bay. Scientists believe that without the Everglades, this reservoir would become salt, and southern Florida as we know it would be no more.

Though it is hardly discernable to the traveler, altitude also plays an important role in the structure of South Florida. From Lake Okeechobee southward, the surface rock slopes like an ever-so-slightly tilting tray to the tip of the state, dropping about a foot every dozen miles. It is down along this crucial slope that the freshwater Everglades "river," as wide as 50 miles and only a few inches deep, flows through sawgrass from the rain-fed lake to the sea. Here and there, scattered limestone outcroppings form the "high-altitude" regions of the Everglades, occasionally attaining a barely noticeable few feet. Through the ages these little hillocks have gathered humus and eventually vegetation, including hardwood trees, to become water-surrounded islands known as hammocks.

To the south of the Everglades, the limestone bed continues on under the shallow waters of Florida Bay, where the centuries have covered it with an overlay of fine mudlike marl. To the west are the Ten Thousand Islands, an ever-changing archipelago of mangrove islets seated on the tops of old sunken sand dunes of the Gulf of Mexico.

The Florida Keys, like the Everglades, lie on a thick layer of limestone. The rock is covered by an ancient coral reef. In the lower islands, the pourous Miami oolite, with its rich vegetation, appears once again. Low-lying islands with slight variations in elevation, the Keys boast a high point of 18 feet, on Windley Key. For the most part, however, they are very flat. There are over 800 islands large enough to appear on government charts, though many other tiny mangrove islets exist and are still aborning. About 30 of the Keys are inhabited.

To the east of the Florida Keys lies the only living coral reef in the continental United States. It is located between four and seven miles offshore, running parallel to the Keys from Key Largo to the Dry Tortugas. This living marine marvel, rising as high as a few feet below the surface of the water and descending to dark depths near the Gulf Stream, protects the Keys from the waves of the pounding Atlantic surf and hence from the development of sand beaches, a great surprise to many first-time visitors.

HISTORY

THE EVERGLADES STORY

Although it took millions of years for the Everglades to evolve, and Indians probably wandered into some of the mysterious interiors for a century or two, the real history of the unique region belongs mainly to the century just drawing to a close. The story of the Everglades is a microcosm of the global story of the interdependence and tensions between mankind and nature, full of despair and promise, of lessons ignored and lessons learned, of life sources and of life itself hanging by a tenuous thread.

Some of the early Indians who roamed coastal portions of the Everglades left a few artifacts and their discarded shells in scattered mounds, but little is known about exactly how they fared in the mosquito-infested, watery environment. Nor is there much evidence that European explorers felt attracted to the marshy tip of Florida, so lacking in solid land and so hostile to travelers. To the casual observer as well as to the ambitious developer, the Everglades long seemed no more than a swamp to be drained and put to better use than nature obviously had in mind. Even as early as 1848, Army and Navy officers chasing Seminole Indians through the muck and swamps returned home stating that the land should be drained for cattle raising and for growing rice, sugar cane, fruits and vegetables. In 1865, a reporter sent to check out post-Civil War conditions in southern Florida commented on the need to get the water out of Lake Okeechobee and the Everglades.

Draining seemed a logical idea at the time and was attempted in little fits and starts as early as the 1880s. But the Everglades were not to be conquered easily. Early attempts were challenged by opponents of taxes and, hence, by lack of money. And whatever progress was made, the task always proved to be much more challenging than originally assumed. In 1905, the state's first comprehensive drainage law was passed, intending to construct a system of canals that would "reclaim" swamp and flood lands. Florida Governor Napoleon Bonaparte Broward, convinced that if enough of the Everglades was drained, the state could grow sufficient sugar to supply the whole country, threw government efforts into the project. By 1909, a canal connecting Lake Okeechobee to Miami was completed, smaller waterways were constructed and drainage for farmland was underway in earnest.

But even this early in the game, occasional critics warned that crucial studies had not been done, that water tables might be threatened, that not enough money was available to fulfill the dreams. But for many years the promises outweighed the criticisms. Southern Florida land sales boomed. Farming got underway. Then World War I put a damper on most of the enterprises. In the 1920s, a couple of devastating hurricanes, several serious fires in the peat-rich regions and, finally, the collapse of the Florida land boom brought a temporary end to state efforts to conquer the mighty Everglades.

At the end of the decade, the Army Corps of Engineers constructed Hoover Dike around Lake Okeechobee, hoping to end the threat of flooding. But again, in 1947, a hurricane caused floods to wipe out farm and grazing lands, proving once again that manmade canals and dikes could not always hold the waters in check. By then, some people began to realize that, though millions of dollars had been spent for drainage and flood control, effective reclamation of the wetlands had still not been achieved. And new problems were appearing as well. Salt began seeping into freshwater sources as water tables were lowered. Fires in the peatlike soils created clouds of smoke that could make eyes water as far north as Tallahassee. Thin layers of soil in land that had been successfully drained and farmed began to disappear. Dry summers pointed up the need for irrigation as well as drainage. A water management district was established in hope of solving some of the problems.

At about the same time as these immediately practical problems were being examined, concerns of a new kind began to be heard. What was all this tampering with nature doing to wildlife, to plant life, to life in general? "Pollution" entered the vocabulary of the concerned, chief of whom was Marjorie Stoneman Douglas, who published her immediate classic, *The Everglades, River of Grass*, in 1947. The good news was that in the same year President Harry Truman dedicated 2000 square miles of the southernmost Everglades as a national park. Here, at last, was an area that could not be touched.

But as fine as the establishment of that important park was, the problems were not over. All the water feeding into the region was, by then, controlled by artificial means. The complex food chain of the Everglades that had always been dependent on natural cycles of rain and drought was now at the mercy of those who manned the pipes and dikes to meet the demands of Florida's evergrowing human population. Two major causeway-style highways, remarkable feats of wetland engineering, now cut across the once-pristine, free-flowing river of grass. Fertilizers and insecticides, so important to farmers but so deadly to many creatures of the wild, also threatened to further upset the fragile balance of nature.

As the problems arose, so did the champions of the preservation of the delicately balanced environment of the Everglades. Sometimes they lost their battles. Sometimes they won, as when they prevented the draining of Big Cypress Swamp, upon which the Everglades is dependent for much of its life, for a mammoth airport. After energetic and skillful protest, the region was turned into a national preserve in the 1970s. But not all the problems have been solved; tensions continue to this very moment.

Some say the Everglades will disappear, that it is too late to turn things around. When the Everglades die, some say, so will all of Florida—Miami, the wildlife, the farms, the Keys and all who are dependent on the irreplaceable water tables that may one day turn to salt. But even with this forecast of doom, tireless efforts continue in search of the perfect balance between humankind and the natural world on which all survival depends.

NATIVE AMERICANS

When the first Spanish explorers approached the Florida shores in the 16th century, a number of native tribes had long resided throughout the peninsula and on its surrounding islands. The southernmost regions were dominated by the Tequestas and the Calusas, who thrived on the abundance provided by the sea and the rich coastal lands. Though the two tribes may have merged from time to time, probably in the Cape Sable region at the tip of the mainland, they were essentially separated by the Everglades. The Tequestas roamed the region from present-day Pompano Beach southward; the Calusas dominated the westward regions from the tip of the peninsula as far north as Tampa Bay and roamed portions of the Florida Keys.

The Tequestas were thought to number only about 800 at the beginning of the historical period. They were great fishermen, usually living near the mouths of streams and enhancing their seafood diet with such varied fare as palmetto berries, sea grapes, palm nuts, prickly pears and venison and turtle meat. They made a flour from the starchy arrowroot plant known as coontie. The Calusas, whose number may have been triple that of the Tequestas, lived principally off the conch, clams, oysters and other shellfish abundant in the Ten Thousand Islands region on the western edge of the Everglades. Though they were not agricultural, some of the early natives often lived in villages and developed a high social structure, thanks to the bounties of nature within their reach. They used wood for ceremonial and practical implements, such as masks, bowls and boats. They made spears and bows and arrows; they designed tools and ornaments from bone and shell.

Like the other early Florida tribes, the Tequestas and Calusas eventually disappeared with the coming of Western civilization and its accompanying diseases and conquering spirit. Some of the void was filled, though, by other natives, Creek Indians who slowly moved into the Spanish Florida territory and down the peninsula from what are now the southern states. They were neither welcomed nor beloved by the European and American settlers. They came to be called "Seminoles," a name perhaps corrupted from the Spanish word *cimarrón*, meaning "wild" or from the Creek words *ishti semoli*, meaning "wildmen" or "outlanders" or "separatists."

By the time Spain finally relinquished Florida to the United States in 1821, one war had already been fought against the Seminoles in an attempt to rid the land of Indians for good. But the Indian "problem" did not go away, so Andrew Jackson, the territory's first governor, declared a second Seminole War in 1835, hoping to quickly remove the annoying offenders to Indian territory west of the Mississippi. The Seminoles proved to be a formidable enemy; the war lasted almost seven years and exacted a great price in dollars and lives. Patrols pushed the Seminoles deeper and deeper into the Everglades. Bounties were offered for the capture of live Indians—$500 for a man, $250 for a woman, $100 for a child. Finally, after seven years of fighting, the backbone of resistance was broken. Following the death of their great leader, Osceola, most of the surviving Seminoles allowed themselves to be "escorted" out of Florida.

But not all of the Indians left. Several hundred disappeared into the Everglades and Big Cypress Swamp, where they spent the remainder of the century living a nomadic life in the wet, lonely region. Like their prehistoric cousins, they lived off the land and sea. They built adaptable stilt houses, called "chickees," safe above the ever rising and falling waters. They developed unrivaled skills of survival in the difficult environment. Their secluded life continued until the building of the Tamiami Trail in the 1920s, when the outside world began to delve into the region.

Not until 1962 did the Seminoles finally resume official relations with the United States, a century-and-a-quarter after their self-imposed independence. Today their descendants, numbering about 2000, live in two separate groups on reservations. Fifteen hundred Seminoles, the Muskogee-speakers, live near Alligator Alley (Route 84) midway between Fort Lauderdale and Naples. A smaller tribe, the Hichiti-speaking Miccosukees, live in a series of little villages along the Tamiami Trail (Route 41) on the northern edge of Everglades National Park, still carrying out remnants of the Everglades lifestyle. Once considered enemies of settlers, these descendants of the Creeks are now accepted as a vital part of southern Florida's rich tapestry.

EARLY KEYS SETTLEMENT

Though they are neighbors, the Everglades and the Keys have very different histories. It helps to remember that in the early days of exploration, the former appeared as an impenetrable swampland, the latter a collection of isolated islands accessible only by boat.

Spanish explorers first sighted the Keys early in the 16th century as they searched for rumored gold and eternal youth. One contemporary chronicler of explorer Ponce de León, observing the chain of islands on the horizon, said they appeared as men who were suffering; hence they were given the name *Los Mártires* or "the martyrs." No one knows exactly when the first European set foot on one of the Keys, but as exploration and shipping increased, the islands became prominent on nautical maps. The nearby treacherous coral reefs claimed many actual seafaring "martyrs" from the time of early recorded history. The chain was eventually called "keys," also attributed to the Spanish, from *cayos*, meaning "small islands."

In 1763, the Spanish ceded Florida to the British in a trade for the port of Havana. The treaty was unclear as to the status of the Keys. An agent of the king of Spain claimed that the islands, rich in fish, turtles and mahogony for shipbuilding, were part of Cuba, fearing that the English might build fortresses and dominate the shipping lanes. The British also realized the treaty was ambiguous, but declared that the Keys should be occupied and defended as part of Florida. The British claim was never officially contested. Ironically, the British gave the islands back to Spain in 1783, to keep them out of the hands of the United States, but in 1821 all of Florida, including the necklace of islands, officially became American territory.

Though most of the Florida Keys remained remote and inaccessible until well into the 20th century, their history glitters with romantic tales of pirates, fortunes gleaned from unfortunate shipwrecks, brief heydays for several island cities, struggling pioneer farmers and occasional military occupation. It also holds its share of tragedy resulting from settlers' encounters with hostile Indians, yellow-fever-bearing mosquitoes, dangerous hurricanes and unpredictable seas.

PROTECTION AND PROSPERITY

By the time of the territorial period, Key West was already recognized as a place with assets. Its proximity to the Florida reef made it a perfect center for the sometimes legitimate, sometimes dubious business of marine salvage. Its deep channels with protected anchorage made it a perfect location for a recoaling station for steamers and a strategic site for a naval base. In 1821, John Simonton bought the island for $2000 from its original Spanish land-grant owner, and the first permanent residents moved in. But by then, pirates had long been reaping great harvests from unfortunate ships in the Gulf of Mexico and West Indies. Pirate history being a colorful blending of fact and myth, in the Keys it rings with names and tales of Black Caesar, John La Fitte, Blackbeard and other nefarious characters who frightened seafarers and buried as yet unearthed treasures throughout the islands.

In 1822, Lieutenant Matthew C. Perry was ordered to take possession of Key West for the United States and to go after the pirates. By the end of the year, 21 American ships cruised the waters in search of pirates, engaging in occasional confrontations. After one fight in which an American lieutenant was killed, a naval base was established at Key West and the fleet enlarged.

But an even more formidable enemy than pirates was yellow fever. In July of 1823 it took the lives of 68 men, causing the Navy to declare the base unfit from July to October. By 1826, the main operations were moved to Pensacola, leaving only coal and supply depots at Key West. The region was still considered to be important militarily, however, a "Gibraltar of the Gulf." In 1845 the War Department announced the building of fortifications at Key West and in the Dry Tortugas; these would become Fort Taylor and Fort Jefferson. Lighthouses had already been sending their beacons from these strategic points for several decades.

Meanwhile, Key West was on its way to its brief heyday as the wealthiest city in Florida. The chief industry was wrecking and salvage. Many 19th-century entrepreneurs were English Bahamians who brought the distinctive speech and architectural styles that would one day become known as "conch," named for the serviceable mollusk that resided in the surrounding waters. Bahamians also profited from the lucrative harvesting of fish and, along with Greek immigrants, high-quality sponges. Cuban migrants arrived with their culture and cigar-making skills; by 1860 a million cigars a years were being rolled in over 150 Key West factories. The salt manufacturing business also achieved high success in the years before the Civil War.

Prosperity was thriving farther up the Keys as well. At the 1836 Constitutional Convention, when Florida became a state, Dade County was established to take in the vast area from Lake Okeechobee to Bahia Honda Key. The inauspicious island of Indian Key was named county seat. Located halfway between Miami and Key West, it was the prime location for wreckers and salvagers, some of whom were purported to be working outside the law, even perhaps luring ships to their dooms on the treacherous reefs.

Whether honest or dishonest, most wreckers did very well and often provided a much needed service to unfortunate captains, crews and shipowners. Indian Key, like Key West, boomed.

But it all came to a tragic halt when, on an August morning in 1840, Indians piloting 17 canoes raided the island, looted and burned crucial stores and buildings and killed several prominent citizens. Four years later, Miami became the county seat, though it would be some time before it reached the former prominence of Indian Key. The final death knell for the wrecking business was the placement of a string of lighthouses to warn sea captains of the dangers of the treacherous reefs.

CIVIL WAR

During the Civil War, though much of Key West's population was loyal to the South, both the city and Fort Jefferson in the Dry Tortugas remained in Union hands. As early as November 1860, a captain of the United States Army of Engineers urged reinforcements so that these two strategic areas of defense would not be lost in case of secession. As the war began, the commanding officer at Key West, determined not to let unfinished Fort Taylor fall into secessionist hands, stealthily led his small force of 44 through a sleeping city to the fort in the dark of night. They set up a defense that the Confederates were never able to capture. Neither of the forts saw any serious action for the duration of the war, though individual blockade runners are thought to have darted about in the waters off the Keys.

Though Fort Taylor and Fort Jefferson became obsolete with the invention of the rifled cannon, the former was noted for the construction of a 7000-gallon-a-day seawater distilling plant and the latter as a dreary wartime and postwar prison. Dr. Samuel H. Mudd was interred at Fort Jefferson for four years because he had unknowingly set the leg of Lincoln's assassin, John Wilkes Booth.

Life apparently went on in the Keys with less distress than in the northern regions of the state. Just after the Civil War, a New York newspaperman was sent to southern Florida to check on postwar conditions. He observed that Key West, Florida's largest town, had grown during the conflict. He said that he had to remind himself that it was an American city, so rich was it in tropical plants and foreign tongues. Later in 1865 observers noted that people living on the Keys had a passion for liquor and wrecking, but they also recorded many citizens engaged in fishing, sponging, turtling and harvesting oranges, lemons, limes, coconuts and grapes.

THE SPANISH-AMERICAN WAR

With its proximity to Havana, Key West and other southern Florida coastal cities took on great importance during the war for Cuban independence from Spain. American sympathy for Cuban patriots was flamed by the publication of a Spanish letter disparaging President William McKinley and by the mysterious sinking of the U.S. battleship *Maine* in Havana harbor on February 15, 1898. The United States demanded that Spain withdraw from Cuba, and, on April 24, Spain declared war. Volunteers, both American and Cuban, signed up to join in the fighting.

The War Department first assumed that Key West would be the principal base for American forces, so civilian, Army and Navy activity increased in the busy city. But Key West lacked sufficient storage space, and its harbor needed improvements such as deepened channels for larger ships; Tampa became the main center of military activity. However, the Navy yard at Key West proved important to the invasion of Cuba. Only 90 miles from Havana, the harbor bustled with freight and passenger boats, newspaper dispatch craft, hospital services, Navy coaling and repair work and Spanish prisoner reception. Forts Taylor and Jefferson were reactivated. Newly installed condensers at the distilling plant were designed to increase freshwater supplies.

The war ended on August 12, but the Army and Navy stayed on to complete important projects in Key West. Improved facilities, beefed-up defenses and deeper channels contributed to both base and harbor.

HENRY FLAGLER'S RAILROAD

By 1896, dreamer, entrepreneur and tycoon Henry Flagler had extended his Florida East Coast Railroad to Miami. In the first years of the new century, homesteaders began settling into the regions surrounding the ever-creeping rails. A town, appropriately named Homestead, sprang up where the railroad stopped in 1904. But Flagler's dream kept steaming forward. In 1905, work began on his remarkable "railroad that went to the sea," an incredible line that traversed islands, spanned inlets and ascended bridges, one of them almost seven miles long, down through the Keys and over the ocean to Key West. On January 22, 1912, the first train rolled into town. Flagler believed that Key West would become a terminal from which passengers and freight would set out across the sea to the south and west. In reality, it became just the end of the line.

Though tourists came to the Keys in impressive numbers and the economy picked up, the glory days were not to last. Key West's great boom began to bust with the beginning of World War I. Tourism was halted. The armed forces were eventually reduced to a garrison. Cigar makers began moving to Tampa. Blight and storm wiped out the sponge beds. Florida's pre-Depression land boom had little effect on the islands, but the ensuing Depression years almost destroyed them. Key West's population declined; debts rose. The government declared a state of emergency.

But the railroad had revealed the potential of the Keys as a tourist attraction. The Federal Emergency Relief Administration of the New Deal undertook to rehabilitate the city. Citizens rallied, many learning to make crafts and novelties from local products or organizing fetes and pageants for tourists. Artists on relief decorated walls and buildings with distinctive murals and other works. The influx of thousands of visitors promised great rewards. But the success was again short-lived.

On Labor Day 1935, one of the severest hurricanes on record destroyed the overseas railroad. Winds raged between 200 and 250 miles per hour. The barometer dropped lower than it had ever registered anywhere before. Near Islamorada, the storm overturned rescue cars with over 400 passengers on board. A camp full of war veterans was destroyed. Whole families disappeared into the sea. Many people predicted this terrible tragedy would mark the end of prosperity for the Keys and moved away. But some long-term residents stayed, determined to rebuild from the rubble of Depression and storm.

MODERN TIMES

When it was discovered that Henry Flagler's railroad had been built on very sound footings, a new dream emerged. Bridges and trestles, undamaged by the storm, became the underpinnings for what would become the Overseas Highway. Old track was recycled as new guard rails for bridges. Flagler's vision of a route across the sea would still be realized, only now the thoroughfare would carry automobiles instead of trains. The first wheels rolled across its new pavement in 1938. Tourists began returning.

Once again, however, the vision of thousands of annual visitors flocking to the tropical islands was dashed, this time with the coming of World War II. But the war did bring the Navy and more improvements to the Keys. A submarine base was built at Key West. A water main, like a new lifeline, began carrying fresh water into the Keys from the mainland. Population again began to grow.

President Harry Truman fell in love with Key West and established his "Little White House" there for regular visits. After the war, artists and writers again began lauding the inspirational ambience of Key West, following such luminaries as Ernest Hemingway, Tennessee Williams and Elizabeth Bishop. Tourists began returning in earnest, attracted by sunsets, seafood, colorful history, beautiful seas and general good times. Gays found the town a comfortable place to establish residency.

The 1962 Cuban missile crisis briefly marred the Keys' positive image, but even that brought a little more military prosperity before most of the Navy finally left Key West for good. In 1980, the Mariel Boat Lift, bringing refugees of assorted backgrounds from Cuba, thrust Key West again into the public eye.

Today, the once-isolated Florida Keys are a tourist and retirement haven, popular with divers and sport fishermen and folks who love the climate and beauty of the place, and who thrive on its relaxed ambience. Though boasting a genuinely slowed-down lifestyle far from big-city hassle and northeastern work ethics, the Keys are no longer free from the influence of the outside world. Drugs and their attendant dynamics, particularly in a region of open southern seas and myriad uninhabited islands, are, and will probably long be, a challenge to law enforcement both on land and in the surrounding waters. Crime happens, as it will, in towns where a comfortable climate makes it easy to live in the streets. And some folks wonder just when the next hurricane will come.

But the mainstay of the Florida Keys is a booming, cheerful tourism. From the retired couple that settles in for the winter with their small RV to the president of the United States, George Bush, who battles bonefish with his longtime Keys' friends, the visitors come year-round. They fish, they scuba dive, they sightsee, they eat seafood, they party, they relax, and some of them stay for good. The Overseas Highway is dotted here and there with clusters of chain eateries and motels that make it look like any-strip-USA. But no matter what kind of resorts are built and how many hamburger places go up, the very nature and location of the Florida Keys will keep them as distinctive from their mainland neighbor as when the Spanish first spotted them across the water.

FLORA

One would need a whole book, or maybe several, to deal fairly with the flora of the Everglades and Keys. Fortunately, both the national park and the state parks, as well as bookstores, provide generous amounts of information to those who are captivated by the plants they discover in these botanically rich environments. The brief entries below can only provide a tantalizing mention of a few of the particular plants that one notices at first glance.

Though many plants are distinctive to the Everglades, one dominates above all others—the finely toothed, one- to two-foot bladed sedge commonly known as "sawgrass." It is sawgrass that makes so much of the Everglades appear as a broad prairie, concealing the shallow freshwater river that runs through it. Green in all but very dry winter months, this sawgrass is one of the oldest plant species on earth.

But though the sawgrass dominates, the Everglades are rich in tropical and subtropical plant life, some found nowhere else on earth. Throughout the vast region, limestone ridges called hammocks rise like little islands in the river of grass, allowing trees to establish themselves above the water line and nourishing a wide variety of flora. Here grow the gumbo-limbo trees, royal palms, wild coffee, mastic, strangler fig, rare paurotis palms and huge mahogony trees. Air plants, including more than a dozen types of bromeliads, thrive among the trees of the hardwood hammocks. So do more than 20 species of wild orchids, some quite rare, and numerous species of exotic ferns and assorted vines.

It is the dwarf cypress, draped with ghostlike Spanish moss, that contributes to the mysterious aura of the Everglades. Despite their stunted size, some of these wispy trees are over a century old. They lose their leaves in the winter, making them appear dead, but they are the hardy survivors of the wetlands. The Everglades also contain forests of tall slash pines that are dependent on the natural, lightning-caused fires to keep their floors clear of undergrowth that might inhibit the young trees. Still, as many as 200 types of plants, including 30 found only here, thrive on the floor of some of the pine forests. Most common is the saw palmetto, accompanied by hardwood seedlings fighting for footings among the pines.

Along the coastal regions of the Everglades and throughout the Keys reside some of Florida's true natives, the mangroves, or "walking trees." Best known is the red mangrove, with its arched reddish roots sprawling out like spider's legs where fresh and salt water meet. A little farther inland the black mangrove sends up its masses of tiny pneumatophores for breathing through the still brackish water. Behind them, the white mangrove and buttonwood thrive on hammocks with other tropical trees.

Mangroves reproduce in an unusual manner. Seeds sprout before they leave the tree to drop into the soft wet bottom or float on the tides to suitable locations where they catch hold and become the beginnings of new islands. Mangroves are useful as well as interesting, stabilizing fragile shorelines, catching the brunt of stormy waves, filtering water, serving as rookeries and shelter for birds and wildlife and supporting diverse marine life with their nutritious falling leaves.

Plant life in the Keys, though much has succumbed to ever-growing development, has much in common with that of the Everglades. In the surviving natural areas grow gumbo-limbo trees, lignum vitae, West Indian mahogony, wild lime and tamarind, Jamaica dogwood and other tropical

(Text continued on page 18.)

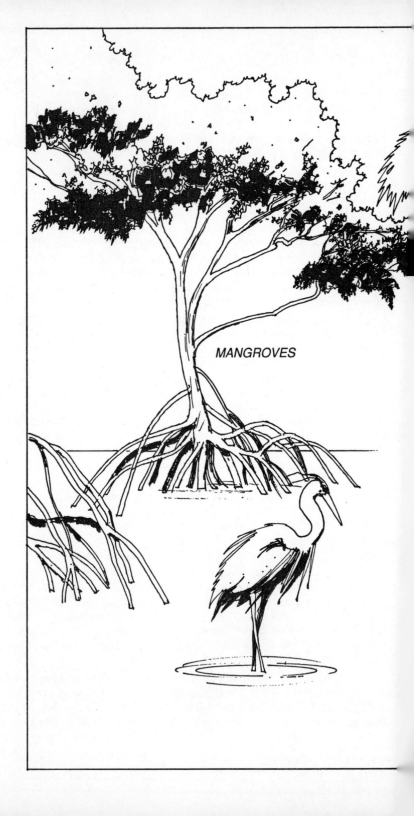

MANGROVES

DWARF CYPRESS
(with Spanish Moss)

ROYAL PALM

SAWGRASS

residents of the hardwood hammocks. Mangroves also abound, creating new keys and enlarging old ones. In the transition zones just above the mangroves can be found the evergreen sea grape, the toxic poisonwood tree, mahoe, cat claw and buttonwood. The slash pine forests of Big Pine Key gave the island its name.

Many of the plants and trees of the Everglades and Keys arrived from the West Indies and beyond, transported on the waves and currents of the sea. Other exotics were brought in by well-meaning (one assumes) settlers and residents. Most notorious of these transplants is the Australian pine (not a true pine) that, though lovely, especially when the wind sings through its branches, has crowded out many native plants and upset natural ecosystems. Tropical fruits, as well as the vast but succulent vegetable farms, have also sometimes flourished at the expense of nature's balance, since they require chemical fertilizers and insecticides for their survival and our dining tables.

FAUNA

An abundance of wildlife resides in the unique subtropical environment of the Everglades. Some species here face extinction, the South Florida wetlands being their only remaining protected home. High on the endangered list is the Florida panther, a rare, seldom seen gray cougar whose number has been reduced to an estimated several dozen, due to the continued loss of habitat. Threatened, too, is the gentle manatee—the harmless, bulky "sea cow"—victim of motorboat propellers and abandoned fishing tackle. Though alligators are the most familiar and easily observed residents of the Everglades, their cousin, the crocodile, struggles for survival in a dwindling habitat (see "Alligators and Crocodiles" in Chapter Two). Facing uncertain futures, too, are the loggerhead and green sea turtles.

But many residents of the region thrive in healthy numbers. Winter's dry season, when they gather at shrinking water holes, is the best time to see them. Exceedingly common, especially around the campgrounds, are the opossum and the raccoon, a paler, smaller creature than his northern cousin. Bobcats appear with some regularity and can sometimes be heard howling on spring and summer nights. White-tailed deer roam freely. The nine-banded armadillo, a native of the Southwest and Central America, has found Florida, including the western Everglades, to be a comfortable home.

Many semiaquatic mammals thrive in the watery environment of the Everglades. Chief among these are the elusive river otter, the endangered Everglades mink, the protected round-tailed muskrat and the marsh rabbit, whose short-eared head is occasionally spied as he pops up on his hind legs on a raised piece of ground to survey his territory.

As one discovers with so much of this subtropical region, it is the visitor who takes plenty of time to explore and examine things closely who reaps the rewards. This certainly applies to those in search of wildlife, for a whole world of miniature creatures resides among the hammocks and prairies. Speedy little lizards of many varieties, colorful grasshoppers and the multi-hued *Liguus* tree snail, as different from one another as snowflakes, are only a sampling of the tiny animals who reside in this distinctive environment. The apple snail is another important resident, being the sole food of the Everglades kite. Photographers find the yellow-and-black zebra butterfly a photogenic delight. The princess of the hardwood hammocks may well be the harmless, showy golden orb weaver, a large female spider whose huge, spectacular webs are so strong that the silk was once used for cross hairs in guns and surveyor's instruments.

Protected natural areas of the Keys are home to many of the creatures that also reside in the Everglades, but the Keys also claim some species unique to these isolated islands. It is believed that some are the genetically changed descendants of creatures who crossed the once low dry land that is now Florida Bay. When the water rose for the last time, they were isolated forever and slowly changed, adapting to their new environment.

Most famous is the tiny Key deer, a miniature subspecies of the main-land white-tailed deer. Residing mainly on Big Pine Key, where they are protected, they are also thinly scattered over more than a dozen other smaller islands. Distinctive, too, are the Lower Keys cotton rat, the Cudjoe Key rice rat, the Vaca Key raccoon, resident of the red mangrove hammocks, and the Key Largo woodrat and cotton mouse who, like the deer, are smaller than their mainland cousins. The endangered Schaus swallowtail butterfly appears occasionally on Key Largo.

Among the reptiles distinctive to the Keys are the mud turtle, the man-grove terrapin and the Florida Keys mole slink, a unique lizard. The Florida Keys ribbon snake, the Big Pine Key ringneck and several distinctive rat snakes also make their homes only on certain islands. A small family of alligators reside in the freshwater pool on Big Pine Key.

Some of the region's most interesting animals reside in the sea. Chief among these are the bottle-nosed dolphin (see "Days of the Dolphins" in Chapter Three) and many species of shark, one of the oldest creatures on earth. Manatees, once abundant in the Keys, are still spotted occasionally. Thirty mollusks, including the two-color crown conch, are among the en-demic invertebrates of the Keys. The great reef that lies beneath the waters of the Atlantic Ocean, parallel to the Keys, is also made up of innumerable animals. For divers and snorkelers and passengers of glass-bottom boats, the reef presents a whole distinctive world of wildlife (see "Kingdoms Under the Sea" in Chapter Three).

(Text continued on page 22.)

SEA TURTLE

MANATEE

KEY DEER

ALLIGATOR

RIVER OTTER

BIRDS

Over 300 species of birds, natives of both the temperate and tropical zones, take up either temporary or permanent residence in the Everglades/Keys region each year. Though the bird population is impressive indeed, it hardly rivals the flocks that caused John James Audubon to feel so astonished, a century-and-a-half ago, that he and his party "could for a while scarcely believe our eyes." Later visitors who crossed the state following the opening of the Tamiami Trail still recall having to wash their cars at the end of the trip, so thick were the birds overhead. Sadly, a big decrease in bird population came about when trendsetters convinced ladies that it was high fashion to wear bird feathers on their bonnets. Flamingo and great white herons and snowy egrets were slaughtered mercilessly; even pelicans and least terns could not escape. Plume hunters hired huge crews to massacre the beautiful birds.

If, as we are sometimes told, 90 percent of the birds are gone, entering the Everglades must have once been an incredible experience, for even the remaining ten percent that soar through the air, perch in the trees and stalk the shallow waters guarantee rewards for even the most casual birdwatcher. In cooler months, one can observe a wide variety without leaving paved paths and roads. Even the uncommon and beautiful roseate spoonbill can sometimes be seen near Flamingo Lodge on the southern tip of the Everglades or among the mangrove shallows beside Route 1 on Key Largo.

In winter, the prime season for birdwatching, endangered woodstorks gather in trees along the Everglades park road and in Big Cypress to fish in the muddy shallows. With binoculars, visitors occasionally observe nesting bald eagles on little islands in Florida Bay and in the Lower Keys. White pelicans ride the winter waves in congenial groups near the Everglades shore.

Peregrine falcons may be spotted along the coasts in spring and fall on their long migrations between the Arctic and South America. Snail kites still nest in the park, and the Cape Sable seaside sparrow makes its exclusive home in the marshes of Big Cypress and the Everglades. And, of course, sea gulls and their assorted relatives, as well as brown pelicans, are part of the coastal scenery year-round.

The most visually exotic birds of the region are those that wade in the shallow waters, standing like beautiful sculptures for hours or stalking their prey with nary a ripple. Most impressive are the great white egrets and the great blue herons, elegant three- to four-foot-tall fishermen. Other easy-to-identify waders include the little blue heron, Louisiana heron, limpkin and the rarer reddish egret. White ibis are common and easy to identify as they bob their bills in and out of the shallows like needles on sewing machines. Magnificent frigate birds nest on the Marquesas Keys in early winter.

Easy to view, too, are many of the water birds, such as purple gallinules, grebes, bitterns, moorhens and marsh hawks. As if they know they are expected to be there, anhingas slice through the water for fish, then hang themselves out to dry in the trees along Anhinga Trail in the Everglades. Cormorants, too, are expert underwater fishermen, darting through the water in great haste and disappearing below the surface for remarkably long periods. On Bush Key, east of Fort Jefferson in the Dry Tortugas, nesting sooty terns from the Caribbean Sea and West Africa are joined by brown noddies and other exotic species in one of the nation's great wildlife spectacles.

Birds of prey include the endangered eagles and snail kites, as well as the swallow-tailed kite and several varieties of hawks, falcons and vultures. Ospreys are especially accommodating to birdwatchers, often building their bulky nests and raising their families on the tops of power poles beside busy Route 1 in the Keys.

Migratory birds, including numerous songbirds, make regularly scheduled visits to the Keys and Everglades. For example, indigo buntings, bobolinks and redstarts appear in the spring. Wintering raptors move in around October. Red-breasted mergansers drop in for their winter stay around November. Prairie warblers, cardinals and common yellowthroats reside in the hardwood hammocks year-round.

Most parks and wildlife refuges provide complete bird lists detailing which species one can expect to observe in a particular region each season of the year. A good bird book is a handy tool for anyone visiting this unique region where one can spot so many species seldom found anywhere else in the country.

NATURAL HABITATS

The Everglades and the Florida Keys contain a variety of habitats, some shared and some distinctive to each region. In this flat, low-lying world, very slight differences in elevation, even an inch or two, can create a dramatic contrast between one region and another. So can other infinitesimal changes, such as water salinity. In this region, human-designed changes—particularly those affecting water supplies—have had devastating effects on the homes and habits of resident wildlife.

The casual visitor to this portion of South Florida can easily learn to recognize a variety of basic habitats:

Pinelands are located on slightly elevated bare limestone outcroppings of the Everglades and on Big Pine Key and nearby islands. These slash pine forests are dependent on occasional fires to keep them clear of competing undergrowth.

(Text continued on page 26.)

WHITE PELICAN

PEREGRINE FALCON

WOOD STORK

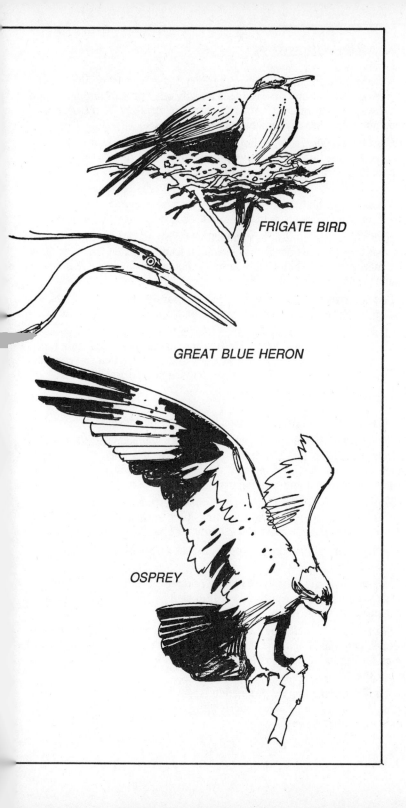

FRIGATE BIRD

GREAT BLUE HERON

OSPREY

Sawgrass Prairies, dominating the Everglades, consist of hundreds of thousands of acres of grasslike sedge and many other grasses through which the freshwater "river of grass" flows almost imperceptibly from Lake Okeechobee and other northern water sources to the sea.

Hardwood Hammocks, rising to as much as three feet, are islands in the "river of grass" on which thrive jungly collections of mahogany, strangler figs, gumbo-limbo, various palms and other trees. This is also where animals find refuge in high-water times.

Heads, soggy leafy mounds that grow clumps of trees, are often named for their individual dominant tree, such as "coco heads" or "cypress heads."

Dwarf Cypress Forests are collections of small, hardy, moss-draped deciduous trees. These open areas of stunted, scattered bald cypress develop where marl and muds build up in solution holes, dissolved cavities in the limestone bed.

Coastal Prairies, appearing like deserts near the sea, are lowlands featuring salt-tolerant plants such as yucca, agave and varieties of cactus.

Mangrove Estuaries are found on the western edge of the Everglades, the Ten Thousand Islands, in Florida Bay and on many of the Florida Keys. These are ever-enlarging collections of salt-tolerant trees that serve as barriers against high seas, residences for microscopic life crucial to the food chain, and rookeries and homes for wildlife.

Freshwater Sloughs, slow-moving, marshy freshwater rivers, serve as reservoirs that are crucial to animals and plants during the dry seasons.

Transition Zones, located between the tidal wetlands and hammocks, are dryland regions that, like the coastal prairies, grow only salt-tolerant vegetation. Beside cacti and unusual shrubs, joewood, silver palm and various hosts to orchids and bromeliads thrive.

Rockland Zones, found on a number of islands, are harsh coastal areas lying between the mangroves and the transition zones and home to buttonwood and saltwort and a few other hardy survivors.

Underwater habitats are an important part of South Florida. These include:

Marine Estuaries, crucial spawning grounds for many types of marine life, harbor abundant varieties of wildlife and, in the Everglades, can be best experienced by canoe.

Florida Bay, the shallow waters between the tip of the mainland and the Keys, contains about one-third of the National Park, including many refuges for nesting and shore birds; manatees, dolphins, turtles, sharks and fish ply the waters.

Sea Grass Beds, highly productive areas of turtle, manatee and Cuban shoal grasses, serve as nursery and feeding grounds for numerous species of fish and invertebrates.

Mud Flats, lining the mangrove hammocks and rocky shores of many islands on both the ocean and bay sides, are flooded at high tide and exposed at low, attracting many shore and wading birds to dine on their supplies of worms, mollusks and fish.

Coral Reefs, considered one of the most complex of all ecosystems, are "underwater gardens" made up of soft animals with hard, stony skeletons. As they die, their skeletal remains become a three-dimensional habitat for thousands of animals and plants ranging from microscopic to gigantic (see "Kingdoms Under the Sea" in Chapter Three).

When to Go

SEASONS

The subtropical Everglades and Florida Keys are warm, aquatic lands with a climate much like the islands of the Caribbean. Winter low temperatures in South Florida average around 60°F with average highs in the upper 70s. Summer average high temperatures reach near 90°, with average lows in the comfortable mid-70s.

There are basically two seasons in this region of far South Florida—winter and summer, or "dry" and "wet." While the Keys, thanks to cooling ocean breezes, are reasonably comfortable year-round, the Everglades are chiefly a winter destination. Winter, the dry season, brings droughts of varying degrees to the Everglades. Mosquito populations drop to their lowest, and birds and wildlife gather at watering holes, to the delight of park rangers and visitors alike. Cold fronts from the north can bring occasional frosts to the Everglades, but generally the weather is mild and comfortable.

In summer, the rains come, completing the annual cycle of drought and flood so necessary to Everglades survival. Great storm clouds gather to drench the land in spectacular afternoon electrical storms that replenish the region and bring welcome relief from hot, humid, steamy days. Biting insects thrive, keeping all but the most hardy visitor from exploring the interior Everglades in summer.

Occasionally the wet season also brings hurricanes; the official season is from June to November. Though they can be devastating, hurricanes need not keep one away from South Florida during these months. Unlike many other weather phenomena, hurricanes come with plenty of warning, allowing visitors either to batten down or depart for inland locations. It's wise to pay attention to warnings and benefit from today's sophisticated meteorology.

In the Keys, winter is usually balmy and dry. Key West has never seen a frost. Though the Keys can get hot on summer afternoons, sea breezes keep the region tolerably comfortable for visitors. Here, too, welcome summer rains cool things off from time to time. Downpours begin and end quickly, with little warning, seldom stopping daily activity. The Keys, long a warm haven for winter-weary northerners, are becoming more and more a year-round destination.

CALENDAR OF EVENTS

JANUARY–MARCH

Key West: A three-month feast of events celebrating the island's rich heritage, **Old Island Days** features house and garden tours, concerts, plays, flower shows, sidewalk art festivals and other happenings.

JANUARY

Marathon: Elizabethan days of yore are recalled at the **Florida Keys Renaissance Faire,** where lords, ladies, knights, jesters and jousting tournaments keep Faire-goers entertained in kingly fashion.

Key West: **The Key West Literary Seminar** celebrates the island's famous role as residence to American literary luminaries with a three-day event featuring a different theme each year.

MARCH

Islamorada: A giant visual-arts display includes original creations of more than 100 artists at the **Rain Barrel Arts Festival.**

Key West: The **Annual Conch Shell Blowing Contest** features the finest conch shell music anywhere; all ages welcome.

APRIL

Islamorada: Complimentary boat rides whisk visitors back 150 years during the **Indian Key Festival** for tours of the little island townsite destroyed by Indians in 1840.

Marathon and Key West: Runners set out for a "marathon" dash over the sea in the annual **Seven Mile Bridge Run,** with fun and frivolity following in Key West at the **Conch Republic Celebration.**

MAY

Marathon: Transforming the Florida Keys' tradition of laid-back angling into a fishing frenzy, the **Marathon Dolphin Scramble** annually assaults the "world dolphin speed-fishing record."

Lower Keys and Key West: The annual **Key West Fishing Tournament** is an eight-month-long event with nine divisions and is held throughout the Lower Keys and off Key West, attracting several thousand anglers annually.

Lower Keys: Innovative self-propelled craft from all over the state compete for prizes in the **Lower Keys Raft Race**, held in conjunction with the **Lower Keys Food Festival**, which entertains with music and tastes of local dishes.

JUNE

Key Largo: Anglers ply the Gulf of Mexico and the Atlantic waters in search of dolphin in the **Key Largo Dolphin Derby,** supporting the area's most important resource—its children.

Key West: Once a part of the July Hemingway Days celebration, the popular **Key West Hemingway Billfish Tournament** now takes place in early June but still recalls the man who made Keys fishing famous.

JULY

Everglades: South Florida ethnic groups join together at the Miccosukee Indian Village for the **Miccosukee Annual International Crafts and Music Festival.**

Lower Keys: Divers glide among the coral heads at Looe Key Marine Sanctuary while listening to an underwater broadcast of classical, semiclassical and contemporary music at the annual **Underwater Music Festival** benefitting marine preservation.

Key West: Storytelling, arm-wrestling, fishing tournaments and lookalike contests highlight the week-long **Hemingway Days,** honoring the memory and the works of the island's most famous literary figure.

AUGUST

Everglades: The **Annual Shark Tournament,** based at nearby Marco Island, promotes awareness of the Ten Thousand Islands with catches and cookouts.

AUGUST–SEPTEMBER

Key Largo: Underwater photographers compete for $10,000 in prizes for photos best exemplifying the splendor of marine life of North America's only living coral reef in the **National Marine Sanctuaries Underwater Photography Contest.**

OCTOBER

Everglades: The **Annual Redfish Tournament,** based at nearby Marco Island, promotes awareness of the Ten Thousand Islands, the Everglades and conservation with lots of festivities.

Marathon: Stalking the elusive bonefish in his shallow-water haunts draws anglers to the **Marathon International Bonefish Tournament.**

Key West: Acclaimed for color, creativity and more than just a touch of satire, the week-long **Fantasy Fest** is Key West's answer to Rio's Carnaval and New Orlean's Mardi Gras.

NOVEMBER

Islamorada: Everyday fishermen team up with film stars, sports figures and famous fishing guides during the **Islamorada Redbone Celebrity Tournament** for a weekend of redfish and bonefish angling and social events benefitting the Cystic Fibrosis Foundation.

DECEMBER–APRIL

Keys-Wide: **The Festival of the Continents** highlights the winter high season with an international performing arts program that includes symphonies, ballet and dance, opera, Broadway musicals, drama, film and art.

How to Deal With . . .

VISITOR INFORMATION

Each chapter of this book lists the chambers of commerce and/or visitor centers that provide tourist and travel information. You can obtain materials on the **Everglades National Park** by writing: Information, Everglades National Park, P.O. Box 279, Homestead, FL 33030 (305-247-6211).

If you need information on the **Florida Keys**, you can call 800-352-5397.

For a free copy of the *Florida Vacation Guide*, contact the **Florida Department of Commerce** (Division of Tourism, Direct Mail Warehouse, 126 West Van Buren Street, Tallahassee, FL 32399; 904-487-1462).

PACKING

Unless you plan to spend your time in South Florida dining in ultra-deluxe restaurants, you'll need much less in your suitcase than you might think. For most trips, all you'll have to pack in the way of clothing are some shorts, lightweight shirts or tops, cool slacks or skirts, a hat for protection from the sun, a pair of quality sunglasses, a couple of bathing suits and coverups, and something *very casual* for any special event that might call for dressing up.

The rest of your luggage space can be devoted to a few essentials that should not be forgotten (unless you prefer to shop on arrival). These include good sunscreens (preferably not oils) and some insect repellent, especially if you are traveling in the summer or heading into the Everglades, even in winter. If stinging jellyfish are a concern, take along a small container of a papain-type meat tenderizer. It won't keep the varmints away, but it will ease the pain should you fall victim.

In summer especially, be sure to take along an umbrella or light raincoat for the sudden showers that can pop out of nowhere. In winter, a sweater or light jacket can be welcome on occasional cool evenings.

Good soft, comfortable, lightweight shoes for sightseeing are a must. Despite its tropical gentleness, South Florida terrain doesn't treat bare feet well except on rare sandy shores or beside a pool. Sturdy sandals will do well unless you are hiking into the Everglades and other wilderness areas. For these forays, you may need lightweight boots or canvas shoes that you don't mind wading in.

Serious scuba divers and snorkelers will probably want to bring their own gear, but it's certainly not essential. Underwater equipment of all sorts is available for rent throughout the Keys. Fishing gear is also often available for rent.

Campers will need basic cooking equipment and can make out fine with only a lightweight sleeping bag or cot and a tent with bug-proof screens and a ground cloth. Because soil is sparse in many campgrounds, stakes that can penetrate rock are a must. A canteen, first aid kit, insect repellent, flashlight and other routine camping gear should be brought along.

Be sure to take along a camera; South Florida sunsets are sensational. Binoculars and a magnifying glass enhance any exploration of natural areas. If you plan to take night walks any distance from the lodge in the Everglades National Park, you will need a flashlight. And don't, for heaven's sake, forget your copy of *Hidden Florida Keys and Everglades*.

HOTELS

Lodgings in South Florida run the gamut from tiny old-fashioned cabins to glistening highrise hotels. Bed and breakfasts are scarce, except in Key West and a few other isolated locations. Chain motels line most main thoroughfares in populous areas, and mom-and-pop enterprises still successfully vie for lodgers in every region. Large hotels with names you'd know anywhere appear in the few centers of size. Schmaltziest of all are the upscale resorts. Here one can drop in almost from the sky and never have to leave the grounds. In fact, you can take in all the sports, dining, nightlife, shopping and entertainment needed to make a vacation complete, although you may miss a fair amount of authentic South Florida.

Other lodgings, such as historic inns that haven't been too spruced up or guest houses where you can eat breakfast with the handful of other visitors, offer plenty of local personality. A few guest houses in Key West cater exclusively to gays. Whatever your preference and budget, you can probably find something to suit your taste with the help of the regional chapters of this book. Remember, rooms are scarce and prices are high in the winter tourist season. Summer rates are often drastically reduced in many places, allowing for a week's, or even a month's stay to be a real bargain. Whatever you do, plan ahead and *make reservations*, especially in the prime tourist seasons.

Accommodations in this book are organized by region and classified according to price. Rates referred to are for the high season, so if you are looking for low-season bargains, it's good to inquire. *Budget* lodgings generally are less than $40 per night for a standard double and are satisfactory but modest. *Moderately* priced lodgings run from $40 to $70; what they have to offer in the way of luxury will depend on where they are located. At a *deluxe* hotel or resort you can expect to spend between $70 and $120 for a double and increase the amenities to include a lobby, dressing room and plenty of space. *Ultra-deluxe* facilities are a region's finest, offering plenty of extras.

If you crave a room facing the sea, ask specifically. Be warned that "waterfront" can mean bay, lake, inlet or even a channel. If you are trying to save money, lodgings a block or so from the water often offer lower rates than those on the edge of the sea.

RESTAURANTS

Eating places in South Florida seem to be as numerous as the fish in the sea, and fish is what you will find everywhere. Whether catfish from the Everglades or yellowfin tuna from the Atlantic, you can almost always count on its being fresh and well prepared. Each season has its specialties, each region its ethnic influences and its gourmet newcomers.

Within a particular chapter, restaurants are categorized geographically, with each restaurant entry describing the establishment according to price. Dinner entrées at *budget* restaurants usually cost $7 or less. The ambience is informal, service usually speedy. *Moderately* priced restaurants range between $7 and $14; surroundings are casual. *Deluxe* establishments tab their entrées above $14; cuisines may be simple or sophisticated, depending on the location. *Ultra-deluxe* dining rooms, where entrées begin at $20, are often the gourmet places; menus may be large or small, though the ambience is almost always casual.

Some restaurants change hands often and are occasionally closed in low season. Efforts have been made in this book to include places with established reputations for good eating. Breakfast and lunch menus vary less in price from restaurant to restaurant than evening dinners. Even deluxe establishments often offer light breakfasts and lunch specialties that place them in or near the budget range.

TRAVELING WITH CHILDREN

Plenty of family adventures are available in South Florida, from man-made attractions to experiences in the wild. A few guidelines will help in making travel with children a pleasure. Book reservations in advance, making sure that the places you stay accept children. If you need a crib or extra cot, arrange for it ahead of time. A travel agent can be of help here, as well as with most other travel plans.

If you are traveling by air, try to reserve bulkhead seats where there is plenty of room. Take along extras you may need, such as diapers, changes of clothing, snacks and toys or small games. If your child has a favorite stuffed animal or blanket, keep it handy.

When traveling by car, be sure to take along the extras, too. Make sure you have plenty of water and juices to drink; dehydration can be a subtle problem, especially in a subtropical climate. Often a simple picnic or a fast-food place with a playground works best at lunch or suppertime, so children can run and stretch their legs. Restaurant dining can turn into a hassle after long hours in the car; it's better to let them have a romp with a peanut butter sandwich in hand.

A first-aid kit is a must for any trip. Along with adhesive bandages, antiseptic cream and something to stop itching, include any medicines your pediatrician might recommend to treat allergies, colds, diarrhea or any chronic problems your child my have.

If you plan to spend much time at the beach, take extra care the first few days. Children's skin is usually tenderer than adults', and severe sunburn can happen before you realize it. A hat is a good idea, along with a reliable sunblock. And be sure to keep a constant eye on children who are near any water.

For parents' night out, many hotels provide a dependable list of baby-sitters. In some areas you may find drop-in child care centers; look in the Yellow Pages for these, and make sure you choose ones that are licensed.

Many towns, parks and attractions offer special activities designed just for children. Consult local newspapers and/or phone the numbers in this guide to see what's happening when you're there.

(Text continued on page 36.)

Keys and Everglades Cuisine

With saltwater on three sides of the Everglades and all sides of the Keys, seafood certainly tops the list of South Florida foods. Add to the saltwater fare freshwater delights from the meandering streams, dark ponds and canals of the Everglades and your fish and shellfish menu has expanded beyond all expectations. Grouper, yellowfin tuna, dolphin (mahimahi), shrimp, spiny lobster and stone crab are only a sampling of the fruits of local seas that offer up particular specialties in every season. From freshwater sources come largemouth bass, catfish and delicate panfish of all sorts.

Each cook seems to prepare seafood dishes in his own way. Heaping fried or broiled platters of seafood are found almost everywhere, but creative chefs also try out unusual seafood recipes with the fervor of marathon competitors. Each region, too, has its own particular specialties, such as fried alligator tail, soft-shell terrapin and frog legs in the Everglades and spicy conch chowder and fritters down through the Keys.

No matter where you live, you may have partaken of South Florida's abundant winter produce. Fat red strawberries, long green beans, prize-winning peppers and tomatoes grow in abundance in the Homestead area. You can often stop at a roadside stand or go into the fields for a pick-your-own sale of whatever is left over from the great quantities shipped across the country. Citrus fruits, from easily peeled tangerines to sweet grapefruit, are abundant in the winter months. Exotic fruits also join the list of South Florida produce, familiar ones such as mangos, avocados and papayas and lesser-known zapotes, lychees and guavas. Coconuts grow in backyards here in the subtropics. Swamp cabbage yields up its heart as the chief delicacy in "hearts of palm" salad.

Everywhere you dine, you will have an opportunity to eat Key lime pie. Basically, it's a simple dessert—a traditional baked pastry pie shell filled with a creamy tart-sweet yellow filling. But how to prepare this

cool delicacy is a hot topic. Purists simply use the juice of the little yellow native limes, a few eggs and some condensed milk. Some say the tradition began when milk had to be canned before the days of refrigeration in the Keys. The limes "cook" the eggs, which may be whole or just yolks. Whether the pie should include meringue is still a debatable issue, as are green coloring, gelatin and crumb crusts. Many visitors have fun trying to locate the restaurant or bakery that serves up "the best Key lime pie."

Conch chowder also has its experts and its history. Queen conchs were once abundant in the Keys and used in all sorts of dishes. Though conchs are now imported, conch chowder is still wonderful, varying from thin and mild to thick and spicy, each cook possessing a favorite secret recipe. Conch is also prepared raw, marinated, in fritters or "cracked" (pounded, dredged in cracker meal and fried).

Native American and ethnic foods have also influenced dining throughout the Everglades and Keys. The Miccosukee Indians along the Tamiami Trail serve pumpkin and fry breads and special Indian burgers and tacos. The Keys' Cuban heritage is reflected in such popular dishes as black beans and rice, *picadillo* (a ground beef dish with capers and raisins), *lechón* (roast pork prepared with garlic and citrus fruits) and *plátanos* (fried bananas). Cuban bread makes Cuban sandwiches a popular lunch meal. The Bahamians are credited with creating a popular fish stew in the Keys and introducing *bollos* (fried balls made of ground black-eyed peas). Flan, a baked custard dessert with a caramel sauce, has its roots in Spain. Guava shells with cream cheese make another popular tropical dessert.

Whether you are sampling conch ceviche or cracking a coconut with a machete (a hatchet will do, of course), you will know that subtropical dining can be very different from eating elsewhere in the country. And very wonderful.

OLDER TRAVELERS

As millions have discovered, South Florida is an ideal place for older vacationers, many of whom turn into part-time or full-time residents. The climate is mild, the terrain level, and many places offer significant discounts for seniors. Off-season rates make the Florida Keys exceedingly attractive for travelers on limited incomes. Florida residents over 65 can benefit from reduced rates at most state parks, and the Golden Age Passport, which must be applied for in person, allows free admission to national parks and monuments for anyone 62 or older.

The **American Association of Retired Persons** (AARP) (3200 East Carson Street, Lakewood, CA 90712) offers membership to anyone over 50. AARP's benefits include travel discounts with a number of firms; escorted tours and cruises are available through **AARP Travel Service** (4801 West 110th Street, P.O. Box 7324, Overland Park, KS 66207).

Elderhostel (80 Boylston Street, Suite 400, Boston, MA 02116; 617-426-7788) offers reasonably priced, all-inclusive educational programs in a variety of Florida locations throughout the year.

Be extra careful about health matters. Bring along any medications you ordinarily use, together with the prescriptions for obtaining more. Consider carrying a medical record with you—including your medical history and current medical status as well as your doctor's name, phone number and address. Make sure that your insurance covers you away from home.

DISABLED TRAVELERS

The state of Florida is striving to make more destinations fully accessible to the disabled. For information on the regions you will be visiting, send for the useful *Florida Physically Challenged Brochure* (Jyl Morris, Department of Commerce, Division of Tourism, 107 West Gaines Street, Collins Building—Room 506, Tallahassee, FL 32399; 904-488-5530).

Everglades National Park (see Chapter Two) has many facilities, including short trails, that are accessible to disabled persons. In Key West, **Holiday Inn La Concha Hotel** (see "Key West Hotels" in Chapter Four) has eight specially designed rooms for the disabled.

For advice on general travel, consult the comprehensive guidebook *Access to the World—A Travel Guide for the Handicapped*, by Louise Weiss (Henry Holt and Company; available from Facts on File, 460 Park Avenue South, New York, NY 10016; 800-322-8755). For information on a sport that's particularly popular in the Keys, you might consult *Scuba Diving with Disabilities*, by Jill Robinson (Human Kinetics Publishers, Box 5076, Champagne, IL 61820; 800-342-5457).

Two federal brochures provide helpful information for disabled travelers. *Access Travel* and *Access to the National Parks* are available from the **U.S. Printing Office** (Washington, DC 20402) for a nominal fee. Also offering information are the **Society for the Advancement of Travel for the Handicapped** (26 Court Street, Brooklyn, NY 11242; 718-858-5483), **Travel Information Center** (Moss Rehabilitation Hospital, 12th Street and Tabor Road, Philadelphia, PA 19141; 215-329-5715), **Mobility International USA** (P.O. Box 3551, Eugene, OR 97403; 503-343-1284) and **Flying Wheels Travel** (P.O. Box 382, Owatonna, MN 55060; 800-533-0363).

The Sporting Life

CAMPING

South Florida offers a wide variety of camping opportunities, from primitive camping in wilderness areas to recreational vehicle parks that resemble fashionable resorts without the condos. Campgrounds in the Florida Keys are often crowded, with sites very close together. For a listing of all the state parks and recreation areas, with information on making reservations, send for the *Florida State Parks Guide* and *Florida State Parks Camping Reservation Procedures* (Department of Natural Resources, Division of Recreation and Parks, 3900 Commonwealth Boulevard, Tallahassee, FL 32399; 904-488-7326).

Everglades National Park (P.O. Box 279, Homestead, FL 33030; 305-247-6211) will send you information on both developed and wilderness camping within the park. **Big Cypress National Preserve** (S.R. Box 11, Ochopee, FL 33943; 817-695-4111) has information on primitive camping opportunities within the preserve. Permits are required for some of the primitive campsites located on keys within **Biscayne National Park** (P.O. Box 1369, Homestead, FL 33090; 305-247-7275).

The **Florida Campground Association** (1638 North Plaza Drive, Tallahassee, FL 32308; 904-656-8878) puts out an annual *Florida Camping Directory* of over 200 private campgrounds and RV parks in the state. Local chambers of commerce also have information on private campgrounds.

Two excellent books for visitors planning to camp in the state are *Camping Guide to Florida*, by Mickey Little (Gulf Publishing Company) and *Florida Parks*, by Gerald Grow (Longleaf Publications).

(Text continued on page 40.)

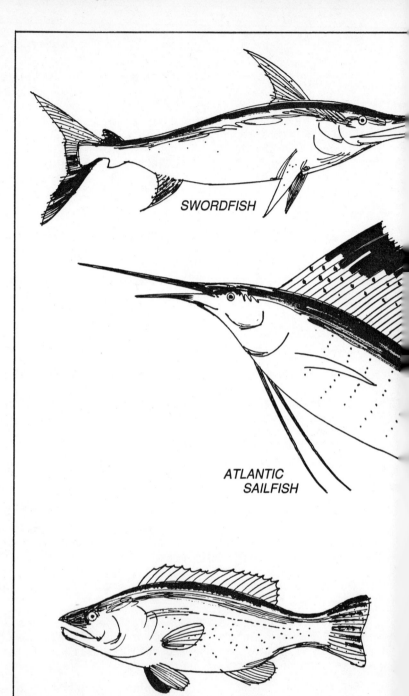

SWORDFISH

ATLANTIC
SAILFISH

LARGEMOUTH BASS

DOLPHIN FISH

WAHOO

YELLOWFIN TUNA

WILDERNESS PERMITS

Backcountry campsites in the **Everglades National Park** (P.O. Box 279, Homestead, FL 33030; 305-247-6211) are accessible by boat, bicycle or foot. A free permit, issued on a first-come, first-served basis no more than 24 hours before the start of your trip, is required and may be obtained at the visitor centers. Permits for wilderness exploration in **Big Cypress National Preserve, Biscayne National Park** and certain state parks may be obtained by contacting the individual sites, as found in the "Beaches and Parks" sections of the regional chapters of this book.

BOATING

From paddleboat to cruise ship, just about every imaginable method of ploughing the waters is available in South Florida. You can bring your own boat if you wish and travel the Intracoastal Waterway or laze away the day on a quiet inlet with a fishing pole. And if you have no boat, you can rent or charter a craft of just about any size or speed. Each chapter in this book offers suggestions on how to go about finding the vessel of your choice. Most marinas and other rental agencies will arm you with maps and advice. Regional chart packets for boaters and divers may be obtained by contacting the **Florida Division of Tourism** (126 West Van Buren Street, Tallahassee, FL 32301; 904-487-1462).

Boating regulations and safety information may be obtained from the **Department of Natural Resources** (Florida Marine Patrol, Boating Safety Program, 3900 Commonwealth Boulevard, Tallahassee, FL 32399; 904-487-3671).

Canoeing is a popular sport in the western and southern Everglades and in several areas of the Keys. To obtain the *Florida Recreational Trails System–Canoe Trails* brochure, contact the **Florida Department of Natural Resources** (Division of Recreation and Parks, 3900 Commonwealth Boulevard, Tallahassee, FL 32399; 904-487-4784). Individual state and national parks also provide canoe trail information.

Houseboating is a lazy, leisurely way to experience the watery wilds in luxury; rentals are available in several regions. Because many interesting destinations are located offshore, tour boats and cruises are also available in numerous regions.

WATER SAFETY

Few places match South Florida for the variety of water sports available. Swimming, scuba diving, snorkeling or just basking on a float are options wherever you can get to the shore. Drownings do occur now and then, but they can be avoided as long as one respects the power of the water, heeds appropriate warnings and uses good sense.

Wherever you swim or dive, never do it alone. Though the surf is seldom high in this region, should the wind whip up incoming waves, keep your face toward them. They can bring unpleasant surprises even to the initiated. If you get caught in a rip current or any tow that makes you feel out of control, don't try to swim against it. Head with it or across it, paralleling the shore. Respect signs warning of undertows.

If you dive or snorkel, practice all the proper techniques and emergency procedures with an expert before starting out. Even professionals consider training updates to be essential for underwater safety. Always display a "Diver Down" flag when in the water, and avoid wearing shiny objects that might attract unwanted sea creatures. Check all equipment prior to any dive, and always dive into the current so it can help you on your return to your boat.

Jellyfish stings are commonly treated with papain-type meat tenderizers. If you go lobstering or crabbing or wading around in murky waters and where shellfish dwell, wear canvas shoes to protect your feet.

Remember, you are a guest in the sea. All rights belong to the creatures who dwell there, including sharks. Though they are rarely seen and seldom attack, they should be respected. A wise swimmer or diver simply heads unobtrusively for the shore or boat. On the other hand, if dolphins are cavorting in your area, don't worry. Dolphins are equipped so as not to run into things, even you, and they may put on quite a show.

Life jackets are a must if you want your boating trip to end happily. This goes for canoes as well as larger and faster craft. Don't mix alcohol and water; excessive drinking is involved in over 50 percent of all drownings and boating accidents. Learn boating rules and obey them; collisions resulting from operator error and high speeds are the primary cause of boating injury.

When swimming and boating, keep your eye on the weather. When electrical storms and high winds are approaching, it's time to head for dry land.

And never, never take your eyes off a child who is near the water, no matter how calm conditions may appear.

Surrounded by so much water in South Florida, the best protection is to know how to swim, and to use your good sense.

WILDERNESS SAFETY

Certain precautions should be taken whenever leaving the main roads and heading into wilderness regions, especially in the Everglades and Big

Cypress. First of all, be sure to let someone know your planned route and schedule before setting out. The biggest problem will likely be biting insects, especially mosquitoes, in all but the coolest winter months. Plenty of insect repellent, long-sleeved shirts, long pants and head covers are the best protection.

Learn to recognize poisonous plants, such as poison ivy, poisonwood and machineel, so they can be avoided. Coral snakes, water moccasins and diamondback and pygmy rattlesnakes do reside in South Florida; by being alert and looking before exploring, you can usually avoid unpleasant encounters. When hiking off the trails, be careful of your footing. Sharp-edged rock, mucky soil and hidden holes can make walking tricky. Check with individual parks and preserves concerning rules for fires and use of off-road vehicles.

FISH AND FISHING

No matter what the season of the year, the Everglades and Keys are an angler's paradise. How you approach the sport is up to you. You can dangle a hook from a cane pole into a sluggish slough or chase bonefish off Islamorada or wrestle with a tarpon on the edge of the Gulf Stream. You can even harvest great rewards by casting your line off an abandoned bridge of the Overseas Highway.

Popular fishing of the Everglades includes both inland waters, where freshwater canals and ponds harbor impressive largemouth bass, black crappie, catfish and bream and other panfish, and the coastal waters of the Gulf of Mexico and Florida Bay. The most sought-after saltwater species here are trout, redfish and snapper. For information on freshwater options, send for the publication *Florida Fishing, Everglades Region* from the **Office of Informational Services** (Florida Game and Fresh Water Fish Commission, Bryant Building, Tallahassee, FL 32301; 904-488-1960). Some areas of the national park are closed to fishing, so it is important to obtain a copy of the regulations from one of the visitor centers or ranger stations before dropping a hook.

Saltwater fishing in the Keys can be roughly divided into three types; reef fishing, offshore fishing (on the oceanside, beyond the reef and out into the Gulf Stream, or westward out on the Tortugas Banks) and inshore and "backcountry" fishing in the gulf and Florida Bay. A monthly publication, *Florida Keys Angler* (P.O. Box 427, Islamorada, FL 33036; 305-664-9660), found at marinas and bait-and-tackle shops, features seasonal information and in-depth fishing articles.

Habitual area fishermen will tell you that there is enough variety in this region to keep you busy and learning for a lifetime, as well as something to catch every day of the year. In the spring, permit, tarpon and bonefish are abundant in the flats, and sharks move into shallow waters to spawn. Spring is also a good time for yellowfin tuna, white marlin, swordfish and snapper. The calm days of summer promise good catches of dolphin (mahi-mahi). As fall days get cooler, action on the reef for snapper and grouper improves; permit, marlin, tuna, wahoo and the challenging bonefish are some autumn rewards. Kingfish show in big schools in the winter; grouper and mackerel fishing also gets underway then. Barracuda and Atlantic sailfish, along with many other species, can be found all year round.

Numerous crustaceans are also harvested from the waters. Perhaps the most popular is the spiny lobster, resident of both bay and ocean. Also delectable is the pugnacious blue crab. Stone crabs are harvested for the meat of their tasty claws, which they graciously grow back after being returned to the water. Shrimp are an important commercial fruit of the sea. Be sure to check on legal seasons and sizes before taking any of these creatures.

If you'd like to try a kind of fishing that is new to you, you will find guide services available just about everywhere boats are rented and bait is sold. Charter fishing is the costliest way to go out to sea; party boats take a crowd but are less expensive and usually great fun. In the ponds and streams of the Everglades region and in the backcountry of Florida Bay, guides can show you the best place to throw your hook or skim a fly. Whatever your pleasure, in salt water or fresh, a good guide will save you both time and grief and increase the likelihood of a full string or a handsome trophy. For those who wish to go it alone in their own boats, there are a number of public access landings throughout the region.

If you go freshwater fishing, you will need a license, and you will have to get it through the local county tax collector. It's easy to do, though, because most fish camps, bait-and-tackle shops and sporting goods stores act as agents. Just look for signs that say "Fishing License for Sale."

For information on saltwater licenses, check at a local marina or with the **Department of Natural Resources** (3900 Commonwealth Boulevard, Tallahassee, FL 32303; 904-488-7236). The **Florida Marine Patrol** nearest the area you are fishing (1275 Northeast 79th Street, Miami; 305-325-3346; or 2835 Overseas Highway, Marathon; 305-743-6542) can also provide you with the latest saltwater fishing facts on licenses, closed seasons and bag and size limits.

There are also fish just to be viewed in the seas of South Florida, especially wherever the living reefs thrive. (See "Kingdoms Under the Sea" in Chapter Three.) Vivid yellows, reds, blues and greens characterize the reef fish, some of which take on almost electric hues. A face mask, with or without a snorkel, will open up an undersea world of incredible beauty and surprises, whether it be along the shore or out among the reefs. In fact, colorful tropical fish may well be some of Florida's loveliest hidden treasures.

TWO

The Everglades

From the air, it seems a vast, mysterious world of land and water at whose edge civilization suddenly stops, a place where no one dwells. From the highway, it appears an endless prairie above which birds fly in winter and clouds build into towering summer storms that flash and crash and deluge the land in torrents. Both impressions are right, but, like the seasonal breezes in this subtropical land, they skim the surface only. For here in the Everglades, perhaps more than anywhere else in the country, the old cliché rings true: there is far more than meets the eye.

In the Everglades, life teems, water flows, creatures struggle for survival in miraculous cycles that have repeated themselves over and over again since prehistoric times. Only today there is one difference. Now the cycles are dependent on humankind, on those who have tamed the waters and channeled the streams and, as a result, now hold the survival of this beautiful, fragile region in their hands.

An understanding and appreciation of the Everglades has come only in recent decades, far too long after the waters that once spilled out of Lake Okeechobee and gently fed this region were diked and rechanneled. For decades, dreamers, developers and farmers were unconcerned about the devastating effects of the changes they so drastically wrought on the natural world of South Florida. To most of them, the Everglades were simply a vast swamp that could be drained and tamed for building and for growing food.

Then, in 1947, Marjorie Stoneman Douglas wrote a book that acclaimed the treasures of this subtropical wilderness, once inhabited only by Indians and home to myriad creatures and plants found nowhere else in the United States. She also struck at the consciences of those who were doing irreparable damage to this region, one whose existence contributed to the life of the whole peninsula. "There are no other Everglades in the world," she began *The Everglades: River of Grass*. "They are, they have always been, one of the unique regions of the earth, remote, never wholly known."

In the same year, President Truman dedicated Everglades National Park. The region has also been designated both an International Biosphere Reserve and a World Heritage Site in recognition of its value as a crucial natural wonder of the world. Although the Everglades actually extend far beyond the park's 2000 square miles, it is in the protected region that visitors can explore the wonders of this world.

At first glance, much of the area looks like inviting prairie that visitors could easily hike through on a nice day. But looks are deceiving. Most of this plain is actually a shallow, gently flowing river, hidden beneath the tall sawgrass and reeds. Except in the pinelands and hardwood hammocks, there is water everywhere. Luckily for visitors, well-designed roads, trails and boardwalks keep feet dry while allowing us to travel through remote areas. And for those who want to explore watery pathways, a number of canoe trails offer adventure into spots accessible only by boat. Bicycling along park roads also lets visitors get closer to nature and discover places that might be missed while traveling in a car.

Three visitor areas lie in Everglades National Park, and each shows a different side of the region's rich character. Shark Valley, the northeastern entrance off the Tamiami Trail, offers tours into the sawgrass prairie, abundant in birdlife and alligators. The northwest Tamiami gateway is at Everglades City, jumping-off place to the Ten Thousand Islands, a Gulf Coast mangrove archipelago popular with anglers and vacationers. The main visitor area, southwest of Homestead, marks the beginning of a 38-mile park road that meanders through sawgrass prairie, hardwood hammock, cypress swamps and lake regions, ending at Flamingo on the edge of Florida Bay. This main road offers access to numerous Everglades habitats via a variety of short and long trails.

Winter is the time to visit the Everglades, the only season when mosquitoes won't eat you alive. In winter you can leave your car, walk the trails, canoe the streams and contemplate the subtle beauty of the place. There are no breathtaking panoramas in this region, where the altitude seldom rises above three feet, but rich rewards await those who take the time to explore. Slumbering alligators lie like half-sunken logs in shallow ponds. Comical anhingas gather on low branches, hanging their wings out to dry after fishing forays. Bird populations are spectacular and diverse, including such easily recognized favorites as roseate spoonbills, osprey, brown pelicans and bald eagles. Subtly colored snails and wild orchids adorn the woods in season. Endangered and rare animals such as the gentle manatee, the Florida panther and the American crocodile, though seldom seen, reside deep within the watery world of the Everglades.

Although well-placed signs explain where to go and what to see, the Everglades are also a region of hidden treasures that will reward all who are willing to quietly search, to wait and watch.

It is almost impossible to visit the Everglades without coming away caring about what happens to this wondrous wet world where life cycles begin and the flow of fresh water keeps the salt of the sea at bay so that cities can survive. One cannot forget Douglas' words: "There are no other Everglades in the world."

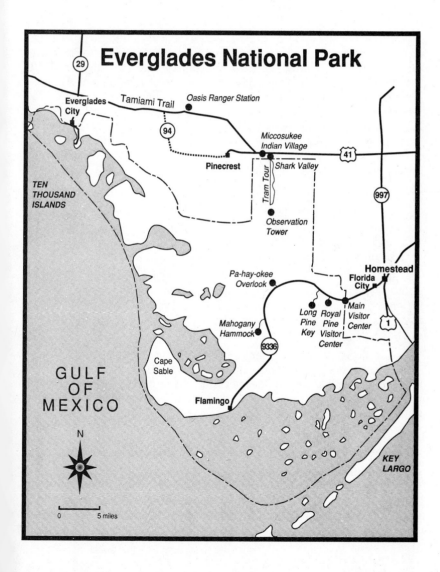

(*Everglades, The Story Behind the Scenery*, by Jack de Golia is a beautifully illustrated, reasonably priced book that introduces many of the Everglades' hidden treasures. You can find it in most area bookstores and gift shops.)

Throughout the text, hidden locales, remote regions and little-known spots are marked with a star (★).

Tamiami Trail Area

Heading westward from Miami, Route 41, known as the Tamiami Trail, provides an almost straight shot from Atlantic to Gulf Coast. For many years, until the building of faster, wider parallel Route 84 (Alligator Alley) to the north, this was the only route across southern Florida. Route 41 plunges through the heart of the Everglades, skirting the northern edge of the **Everglades National Park** and cutting through the southern portion of the **Big Cypress National Preserve**. Though not wildly scenic, it is an intriguing road, traveling through miles and miles of what the Indians called *pa-hay-okee*, or "grassy water." Sometimes canals parallel the narrow highway, their banks busy with people fishing with cane poles. In other places Australian pines grow so tall and full that they have been repeatedly trimmed to form a half-roof over the road. But mostly the landscape is sawgrass prairie, with the great, wide, almost-hidden river running imperceptibly through it. Drivers are instructed to travel this road with lights on at all times, a safeguard against possible tedium and the strange effect the region seems to have on one's depth perception when contemplating passing.

A few entrepreneurs have set up shop along the Tamiami Trail, mostly in the business of airboat rides, which environmentalists frown upon. For the most part, however, the highway, while a masterful engineering feat in its day, is a lonely one, blessedly short on billboards and long on Everglades mystique.

Part of that mystique is conveyed by the region's only human inhabitants, the Miccosukee Indians. Although they trace their ancestry back to centuries before the United States became a nation, the Miccosukee were not recognized as a tribe by the federal government until 1962. About 500 of them now live on a reservation along Route 1. They are descendants of a group that successfully hid in the Everglades during the period when Florida's Indians were being rounded up and sent west. You can visit the designed-for-tourists **Miccosukee Indian Village** (Route 41, 25 miles west of Miami; 305-223-8388; admission) for a guided or self-guided tour that includes a museum, cooking and living chickees (palm-thatched native houses), a nature walk, craft areas, a shooting gallery and an arena where you can watch alligator wrestling. Nearby, the **Miccosukee Airboat Rides** offer noisy, environmentally questionable trips over the sawgrass deeper into the Everglades; the longer rides include a stop at an old hammock-style Indian camp.

The 15-mile, two-hour tram tours offered in the **Shark Valley** (Route 41, 30 miles west of Miami; 305-221-8776) section of the Everglades National Park acquaint visitors with the heart of the sawgrass region. Stops are made along the way to spot birds or alligators, and for lessons on the park's hydrology, geology, vegetation and wildlife. Time is also allowed for climbing the 65-foot observation tower, which provides excellent views of the vast wetlands. Sightseers may also travel the tram road on foot or bicycles, which are rented at the entrance.

Where Route 41 veers northwestward, you can head straight and take a scenic detour on **Route 94,** which travels deep into cypress and pineland backcountry on its way toward Pinecrest. This is called the "loop road," but unless you have a four-wheel drive vehicle, you would do best to turn back when the road begins to deteriorate, about eight miles in, near an interpretive center.

Back on Route 41, northwest of Shark Valley, you will enter **Big Cypress National Preserve**, 2400 square miles of subtropical Florida swampland vital to the preservation of the Everglades. To get an idea of Big Cypress' importance and beauty, stop at the **Oasis Ranger Station** (813-695-2000) and see the excellent audiovisual introduction to this crucial region.

Though not encouraged by the National Park folks because of their noise and impact on the fragile environment, airboats and swamp buggies are popular with tourists. **Wooten's** (Route 41, Ochopee; 813-695-2781; admission) offers these rides all day long, carrying visitors away from the highway into the deeper regions of the Everglades. A number of private individuals also offer rides; you'll see their signs along the road.

Slow down as you come up to the microscopic community of Ochopee, or you might miss "the smallest and most photographed post office in North America." You'll know it by the American flag, the blue letter box, the sign that reads **Post Office, Ochopee, FL** and all the tour buses disgorging passengers so that they can go into the tiny frame building and get their letters stamped.

By turning south on Route 29, you can reach the entrance to the eastern edge of the Everglades National Park, at Everglades City. Stop at the **Everglades City Chamber of Commerce** (Routes 41 and 29; 813-695-3941) to pick up information about this little town and the neighboring region.

At the privately owned **Eden of the Everglades** (Route 29, two miles south of Route 41, Everglades City; 813-695-2800; admission) you can ride the quiet *Jungle Queen* tour boat to observe some of the flora and fauna of the area in a natural setting. With the ticket, you also get to visit Eden's swamp-style zoo for closer looks at some of the region's wildlife.

Continue south to the **Everglades National Park Visitor Center** (Route 29, south of Everglades City; 813-695-3311). Here you can obtain information about the western regions of the park, including the **Ten Thousand Islands** area. The **Everglades National Park Boat Tours** (Visitor Center; 813-695-2591) cover portions of this territory on the Gulf of Mexico, informing visitors how the mangrove islands are formed and acquainting them with the resident wildlife, especially shore and wading birds. Endangered American bald eagles, gentle manatees and playful dolphins often reward the sharp-eyed explorer. Some of the tours make stops on a small gulf island for shelling and a guided walk.

Nature trips by boat into the Ten Thousand Islands area are offered by **Captain Dan** (Chokoloskee Island; 813-695-4573). **Island Charters** (Chokoloskee Island; 813-695-2286) offers nature trips especially geared to photographers and birdwatchers.

Chokoloskee (Route 29, across the causeway south of Everglades City), a small island filled with motor homes, cottages and little motels, is a popular spot for visitors wishing to fish the Ten Thousand Islands region. It also has the distinction of being built on a gigantic shell mound created by early Indians.

To see the Everglades from the air, you can hop aboard one of **"Happy Harry's"** Scenic Airplane Rides (Everglades City Airport; 813-695-4211). You will discover that, despite its tremendous size, the national park is only a portion of the Everglades. From the air, too, you will realize what a watery, remote area this really is. Scenic airplane rides are also offered by **Everglades Aviation** (Everglades City Airport; 813-695-3174). They will take you over the Ten Thousand Islands and arrange seaplane trips to the Dry Tortugas, west of Key West.

After you leave the park's western area, you can travel seven miles west of Route 29 on Route 41 to get to **Fakahatchee Strand State Preserve** (813-695-4593), the major drainage slough of the Big Cypress Swamp (see "Tamiami Trail Area Beaches and Parks" in this chapter). You can walk the boardwalk through the tall, dense, swamp forest of royal palm and bald cypress and admire the numerous orchidlike air plants that are said to grow only here. Rangers conduct regular "wet" walks into the swamp to see other rare plant life.

Island Nature Cruises (Port of the Islands, ten miles northwest of Everglades City; 813-394-3101) explore about 14 miles of the mangrove mazes, broad bays and sandy beaches of the Ten Thousand Island region of the western Everglades.

Collier-Seminole State Park (Route 41, 20 miles northwest of Everglades City; 813-394-3397; admission) offers a good introduction to the vegetation and wildlife of the western Everglades (see "Tamiami Trail Area Beaches and Parks" in this chapter). Besides interpretations of the natural world of rare Florida royal palms, tropical hammocks, cypress swamps, salt marshes and pine woods, there is a replica of a blockhouse used in the Second Seminole War and a display of a "walking dredge" used to build the Tamiami Trail.

If your trip takes you northwest from Everglades City to Naples (via Route 41) or due north to Immokalee (via Route 29), detour to **Corkscrew Swamp Sanctuary** (★) (Sanctuary Road off Route 846; 813-657-3771; admission) for another excellent and easy foray into the Everglades. The National Audubon Society saved this 11,000-acre reserve from foresters in the 1950s; it now serves to protect endangered wood storks and other species. A mile-long boardwalk leads through lakes of lettuce fern and a broad variety of Everglades ecosystems.

TAMIAMI TRAIL AREA HOTELS

If you prefer to stay close to the western park area, try the **Captain's Table Resort** (Route 29, Everglades City; 813-695- 4211). This large resort offers hotel rooms and suites in its main lodge and one- and two-bedroom villas, some featuring screened decks. There is a restaurant and lounge, a large pool and a complete marina. Boat tours of the Ten Thousand Islands are available; good beaches are only five miles away—by boat. Moderate to deluxe.

The **Rod and Gun Lodge** (200 Riverside Drive, Everglades City; 813-695-2101), a 1920s-era hunting and fishing club, no longer rents rooms in the lodge itself. You *can* sit on its airy screened porch or admire the mounted game fish and red cypress paneling of the massive old lobby. And you can stay in the rather ordinary cottages on the grounds, swim in the screened-in, heated pool, play tennis or shuffleboard and feast in the lodge's huge dining room. Complete docking facilities alongside attract some pretty impressive boats. Moderate.

Outdoor Resorts (Route 29, Chokoloskee Island; 813-695-2881) is basically an RV park that takes up a goodly portion of this small island, but if you stay in one of their eight motel units or rent one of their RVs you can take advantage of all the resort amenities. The units are tiny and neat with modern kitchenettes; on the grounds are a restaurant, health spa, pool and tennis courts. Bicycle and boat rentals are available. Rates are moderate for both motel efficiencies and RV rental trailers.

There are also a few small mom-and-pop motels in Everglades City and on Chokoloskee Island. They are very simple but convenient for folks who just come and fish.

If you are seeking the amenities of a full-service resort while exploring the western Everglades, try **Port of the Islands** (25000 Tamiami Trail East [Route 41], Naples; 813-394- 3101) about 15 miles northwest of Everglades

City. Residing on 500 acres and surrounded by parklands, the resort offers hotel rooms and efficiencies for deluxe to ultra-deluxe rates. You can keep yourself busy with golf, skeet and trapshooting, swimming, dining, spa and health club activities, and nature cruises and guided fishing trips into the Ten Thousand Islands. The freshwater river that flows through the grounds feeds a harbor that has been designated a manatee sanctuary.

TAMIAMI TRAIL AREA RESTAURANTS

The **Miccosukee Restaurant** (Route 41, Miccosukee Indian Reservation; 305-223-8388) is a typical roadside restaurant with strip-steak/fried-fish fare. But the local Indians who own and operate this place add their own special dishes to the menu—good things such as pumpkin bread, fry bread, Miccosukee burgers and tacos, and catfish caught in the Everglades. It's the best place to eat while traveling the Tamiami Trail. Budget to moderate.

Along with the usual fried and broiled seafood, you can try such delicacies as 'gator tail, cooter (freshwater soft-shell terrapin) and pan-fried venison at the **Oyster House** (Route 29, Everglades City; 813-695-2073). Ships' wheels and other nautical paraphernalia create a very pleasant, informal seaside atmosphere. Moderate.

The menu at the **Rod and Gun Club** (200 Riverside Drive, Everglades City; 813-695-2101), like those at so many area eateries, features frog legs, stone crab claws and native fish in season, but the ambience is unlike any other in far South Florida. You may dine in the massive, dark, cypress-paneled dining hall of this once-elegant old hunting and fishing lodge or be seated on the airy porch, where you can have a splendid view of the yachts and other fine boats that dock a stone's throw away. The selection of seafood, steak and chicken is small but well prepared. Moderate to deluxe.

The Captain's Table (Route 29, Everglades City; 813-394-5700) offers a nice assortment of local seafood, frog legs and a few veal and beef dishes. It's the setting that's especially fun, for the restaurant is located in the old yellow-stuccoed, tile-roofed, Spanish-style railroad station. Right on the edge of an inlet, the place actually has the feel of a ship, with high arched windows offering a broad, watery view and a lounge that's the hull of a carved wooden galleon. Moderate to deluxe.

TAMIAMI TRAIL AREA SHOPPING

Along with the usual souvenirs, you will find handcrafted baskets, jewelry and the intricate, colorful patchwork clothing for which the Miccosukee

Indian women are famous, at the **Miccosukee Indian Village Gift Shop** (Route 41, 25 miles west of Miami; 305-223-8388).

If you are a souvenir hound, stop at **Wooten's** (Ochopee; 813-695-2781) and you'll never have to go anywhere else for those plastic flamingos and vinyl alligators.

TAMIAMI TRAIL AREA NIGHTLIFE

One Everglades City resident explained, "We don't have much nightlife here, and we like it that way!" So unless you can be contented with the dark, tropical night and the jungle sounds, you'll usually have to head up to Naples and beyond for bright lights.

"The Glassroom" at the **Oyster House** (Route 29, Everglades City; 813-695-2073) does have local bands and dancing on Friday and Saturday nights.

TAMIAMI TRAIL AREA BEACHES AND PARKS

Shark Valley/Everglades National Park—This public access to the park features a 13-mile loop road that delves deep into the sawgrass expanses of the Everglades. Because no private vehicles are allowed in this protected region, you must visit either on foot, by bicycle or via one of the open-sided trams. (See "Tamiami Trail Area" in this chapter.)

Facilities: Picnic area, restrooms, vending machines, hiking and biking trail, nature trail, bicycle rentals, tram rides; information, 305-221-8455.

Getting there: Off Route 41, 35 miles west of Miami.

Everglades City/Everglades National Park—This entrance to the park allows access to the vast, ever-changing Ten Thousand Islands, a mangrove archipelago that serves as both a nesting grounds for birds and a nursery for sea life. Sport fishing is the region's greatest drawing card, but visitors can also take guided boat tours to observe dolphins, manatees and birds and to visit shelly island beaches and learn of the Indians who once fished these waters and left their shell middens and a few artifacts to attest to their presence. The 99-mile Wilderness Waterway, popular with experienced canoeists, twists through marine and estuarine areas all the way to Flamingo at the tip of the state. Several area rivers offer shorter canoeing opportunities.

Facilities: Visitor center, restrooms, concession stand, boat tours, canoe rental; information, 813-695-2591. *Fishing:* Excellent for such favorite saltwater fish as snapper, redfish and trout. *Swimming:* Not recommended, except on certain island locations accessible only by boat.

Getting there: Entrance on Route 29 off Route 41 at Everglades City.

Big Cypress National Preserve—A 2400-square-mile area of subtropical Florida known as Big Cypress Swamp makes up this preserve. Its establishment reflected a serious concern for the state's dwindling wetlands and watersheds, especially those affecting Everglades National Park. Created in 1974, this wilderness area of wet and dry prairies, coastal plains, marshes, mangrove forests, sandy pine woods and mixed hardwood hammocks has few facilities for visitors. It exists to protect the abundant wildlife living here and the watershed, which will be needed by future South Florida generations. Visitors can hike along a trail through the preserve.

Facilities: Picnic tables at several roadside parks, restrooms at the ranger station; information, 813-695-2000. *Camping:* Primitive camping allowed.

Getting there: Located on Route 41 between Shark Valley and Everglades City.

Fakahatchee Strand State Preserve—This strand, the drainage slough for the Big Cypress Swamp, is the largest and most interesting of these natural channels cut by the flow of water into the limestone plain. The slough's tall, dense, swamp forest stands out on the horizon in contrast to the open terrain and sawgrass plain around it. Its forest of royal palms, bald-cypress trees and air plants is said to be unique on earth. Approximately 20 miles long and three to five miles wide, the preserve offers visitors views of some of its rare plant life, including a wide variety of orchids. Rangers conduct regular "wet" walks into the swamp to see other unusual plant life.

Facilities: Interpretive trail and boardwalk; for information, call 813-695-4593.

Getting there: Located 11 miles northwest of Everglades City on Route 41.

Collier-Seminole State Park—The wildlife and vegetation of this park are representative of the Everglades region with tropical hammocks, salt marshes, cypress swamps and pine flatwoods. A number of endangered species, such as Florida black bears, crocodiles and Florida panthers, are protected, and sometimes spotted, in this rich and diverse region. On display are a "walking dredge" used to build the Tamiami Trail and a replica of a blockhouse from the Second Seminole War. A limited number of visitors each day are allowed to canoe into the park's pristine mangrove swamp wilderness preserve, a 13.5-mile trip.

Facilities: Picnic areas, restrooms, nature trail, hiking trail, canoe rental, boatramp, interpretive center; information, 813-394-3397. *Camping:* Permitted. *Fishing:* Saltwater, for mangrove snapper, redfish and snook.

Getting there: Located about 20 miles northwest of Everglades City on Route 41.

Main Visitor Area

Early settlers came to Homestead to cultivate the rich land that was slowly "reclaimed" from the swampy Everglades. They planted and harvested vegetables and citrus and other tropical fruits suited to the far South Florida climate. Much of the area is still agricultural today, a winter fruit and vegetable basket that feeds people all across the country. The Homestead/Florida City area is also a crossroads of sorts. Miami, to the north, is close enough that some of Homestead's street numbers are continuations of those in the big city, and crime is a problem from time to time. Head southeast and you are on your way to the Florida Keys. Due east is Biscayne National Park, a mostly underwater preserve of sea and reef and islands that are an upper continuation of the Keys but accessible only by boat. To the west is Everglades National Park, the main section where visitors can travel a 38-mile road all the way to Florida Bay and experience the many wonders of this exotic landscape.

If you want to begin your exploration in the Florida City/Homestead area, don't forget to stop at the very fine **Visitor Center** at Florida City (160 Route 1; 305-245-9180). Here you can obtain information about the main public portion of Everglades National Park as well as a number of other places to see and things to do in the area.

Sightseeing tours of this South Florida region are offered by **Trolley'n Along Tours** (22400 Route 1, Goulds; 305-258-3414). This company tours local sites, farms and historic buildings; special tours may also be arranged for as far away as Everglades City.

There is a lot to be seen off the Atlantic coast east of Florida City in **Biscayne National Park**, most of it underwater (see "Main Visitor Area Beaches and Parks" in this chapter). But even if you are not a snorkeler or scuba diver, you can get an excellent view of the nearby coral reef from the **glass-bottom boat** that departs from park headquarters at Convoy Point. Daily trips to the reef, as well as island and bay cruises, are offered by **Biscayne Aqua Center** (Biscayne National Park Headquarters, end of 328th Street, east of Florida City; 305-247-2400).

Lovers of orchids and all things beautiful should not miss **Fennell's Orchid Jungle** (26715 Southwest 157th Avenue, Homestead; 305-247-4824; admission). Over 100 different orchids are native to Florida, and they make up only a small portion of the over-12,000 varieties you'll find in this wonderful jungle hammock.

The **Preston B. Bird & Mary Heinlein Fruit & Spice Park** (24801 Southwest 187th Avenue, Homestead; 305-247-5727; admission) is a 20-acre random grove planted with over 500 varieties of fruit, spices and herbs from around the world. Visitors are invited to stroll among the citrus, banana, lychee, mango, starfruit and other tropical trees.

South of Homestead, the cultivation suddenly stops, and **Everglades National Park** begins, almost like a boundary of uneasy truce between man and nature. You quickly forget that Miami is just up the road a piece or that tended gardens lie behind you. Before you lies the mysterious world of what some call "the real Florida," the home of the alligator, the panther, the royal palm and the flamingo.

There are a number of ways to tackle the main visitor area of the park. For help in designing your plan, stop at the **Main Visitor Center** (11 miles southwest of Homestead; 305-247-6211) just before entering the gate. Here park staff members will provide you with all sorts of helpful information, including weather, trail and insect conditions and listings of the season's varied and informative ranger-guided tours. A fine audiovisual presentation and a wide assortment of books provide good introductions to the area.

Once you have paid your admission and entered the park, you are on the single park road that will eventually arrive at Flamingo, 38 miles away, at the tip of the state on the edge of Florida Bay. This winding, lonely road traverses the heart of the park, meandering among tall pines, through seemingly endless expanses of sawgrass prairie and alongside mysterious dark ponds. Off this road lie a number of paths, trails, boardwalks and waterways designed to give the visitor as wide an Everglades experience as possible. Some of the trails require only short strolls of half-a-mile or less, but they reward with close-up views of a great range of environments and inhabitants. Because so much of the terrain is submerged in water, it is wise to stick to the paths provided unless you go exploring with a park ranger.

Right inside the park entrance, watch for signs to the **Royal Palm Visitor Center** on your left. Even if you have already spent a good amount of time at the main center, you would do well to take a stroll down each of the two half-mile trails that begin here. Close together but very different, each plunges into a distinctive Everglades environment. Interpretive signs help you notice things you might otherwise miss, such as how the strangler fig got its name or why alligators are so vital to the survival of the region.

The **Anhinga Trail** travels a boardwalk across Taylor Slough, a marshy pool that attracts winter birds and other wildlife that assemble with apparent unconcern for the season's thousands of visitors with cameras and zoom lenses. This is a perfect spot for viewing alligators and numerous water birds, including the comical anhinga as he perches on a branch and hangs his wings out to dry. Here, too, you can gaze across broad vistas of sawgrass prairie.

Nearby, the **Gumbo-Limbo Trail** leads through a jungly tropical hardwood hammock rich in gumbo-limbo, strangler fig, wild coffee, royal palms and other tropical trees as well as numerous orchids and ferns. Air plants and butterflies often add to the beauty of this spot; interpretive signs help visitors get acquainted with tropical flora that will occur again and again throughout the park.

About six miles from the main entrance, the half-mile **Pineland Trail**, near a camping area at Long Pine Key, circles through a section of slash pine forest. Here the ground is dry; occasional fires keep undergrowth in check so the pines can thrive without competition. This is a good place to get a look at the rock and solution holes formed in the shallow bed of limestone that lies under South Florida. Or just to picnic beside a quiet lake. For a view of pinelands closer to the park road, stop at the **Pinelands** sign about a mile farther on.

As you continue down the park road and gaze across the sawgrass prairie, you will notice stands of stunted trees that, during winter, appear dead or dying, since they are hung with moss from ghostlike gray branches. These are bald cypress, which thrive in watery terrain but remain dwarfed due to the peculiar conditions of the Everglades. In spring they put out lovely green needles. Some that you see, although dwarfed, have been growing here for over a century.

About six miles beyond the Pinelands, you come to the **Pa-hay-okee Overlook**, named for the Indian word for Everglades, meaning "grassy waters." Walk the short boardwalk and climb the observation tower for a wonderful panorama of the sawgrass prairie dotted with collections of ancient dwarf cypress and small island hammocks of hardwoods. This is one of the best overviews in the park; it's a great place for birdwatching.

Some park rangers refer to hammocks as the "bedrooms of the Everglades," the places where so many wild creatures, large and small, find dry ground and shade from the tropical sun. About seven miles from Pa-hay-okee, you can explore one of these magnificent "highlands" that thrive just above the waterlines. The half-mile **Mahogany Hammock Trail** enters the cool, dark, jungly environment of a typical hardwood hammock, where you'll find rare paurotis palms and large mahogany trees, including one said to be the largest mahogany in the United States. Look and listen closely— barred owls, golden orb spiders, colorful *Liguus* tree snails and many other creatures make their homes in this humid "bedroom."

From Mahogany Hammock the park road heads due south through stands of pine and cypress and across more sawgrass prairie. You are now nearing the coast and will begin to see the first mangrove trees, evidence of the mixing of salt water from Florida Bay with the freshwater that flows from the north. You will pass several canoe-access spots along the road here, including the one at West Lake, about 11 miles from Mahogany Hammock.

Stop at the **West Lake Trail** for a good close-up look at mangroves. You can walk among the four species that thrive here along the half-mile boardwalk trail. With a little practice you will be able to identify them all— the predominant red mangroves with their arched, spidery prop roofs, black mangroves sending up fingerlike breathing tubes called "pneumatophores" from the mud and white mangroves and buttonwood on the higher, dryer shores of the swampy areas. The West Lake shoreline is one of many im-

(Text continued on page 60.)

Alligators and Crocodiles

Stroll the boardwalk of Anhinga Trail, take the loop tour in Shark Valley or explore many of the other paths in the Everglades National Park and you will be certain to see the area's chief resident, the American alligator. Like dark, greenish-black, lifeless logs, they often lie basking motionless on the sunny banks of water holes or glide through ponds and sloughs with only their nostrils and eyes breaking the surface.

Once hunted for the stylish shoes, boots, luggage and pocketbooks produced from their tough hides, or for the slightly chewy, chicken-flavored tail meat, alligators are a now a success story of preservation. Classified as endangered and protected by law for several decades, their once perilously low population has recovered so well that alligators are once again a common sight in the Everglades. They appear in many other parts of Florida as well, occasionally to the distress of nearby human residents. While man's encroachment still takes its toll on this ancient creature, the comeback has been so dramatic that the alligator has been reclassified from endangered to threatened.

The American crocodile has not been so fortunate. Only a few hundred are believed to remain in Florida, and they are rarely seen. However, the sign along Route 1 on the way to Key Largo warning "Crocodile Crossing" can be believed. Regular drivers of this road claim to have occasionally spotted the reptiles, who make their homes in this marshy region. Lighter in color than alligators, crocodiles possess narrower, more pointed snouts than their cousins. They can also be identified by a long lower fourth tooth that protrudes impressively when the jaw is closed. Occasionally growing to lengths of 12 feet, they are considered to be more aggressive than alligators.

But one should not be misled by the seeming docility of the Everglades alligator. An active predator, the alligator roams freely in search of food and will eat anything from turtles to wading birds to unlucky mammals trespassing its territory. Females build impressive nests, piling up mud and

grass and debris to as high as six or eight feet. Here they lay their eggs, which the sun and decaying mulch will hatch after about nine weeks. The alligator is a good mother, staying nearby so she can care for her young as soon as the eggs hatch. Male alligators can measure up to 14 feet in length, though most adults average between six and ten feet.

Of particular importance is the alligator's role as the "Keeper of the Everglades." Getting ready for the region's annual dry season, the alligator prepares its own water reservoirs by cleaning out large solution holes, dissolved cavities in the limestone bed of the Everglades. As the rains decrease, these "'gator holes" become important oases for all manner of wildlife. Fish, snails, turtles and other freshwater creatures seek refuge in the pools. Here many will survive until the rains return, when they will leave to repopulate the Everglades. Others will serve as food and sustenance for resident mammals and birds, as well as for the accommodating, future-thinking alligator. This role has made the alligator's comeback particularly important to the continuing life cycles of the Everglades.

While alligators are generally not considered dangerous to humans, warnings for avoiding close contact should be taken seriously. Tragic accidents do happen from time to time, particularly when people carelessly trespass in an alligator's territory. These reptiles are known to be especially aggressive during the spring breeding season, and mothers remain protective of their young for quite some time.

But alligators are certainly the chief attraction of the Everglades, and the national park has designed a number of excellent observation points in a variety of habitats. A small family of alligators also reside at **Blue Hole** (2.25 miles north of Route 1 on Key Deer Boulevard) on Big Pine Key in the lower Florida Keys.

Crocodile and alligator ancestry reaches back millions and millions of years. Viewing them, one is looking back into another time. Though their surroundings may have changed greatly, these creatures and their habits and habitats have not.

portant spawning grounds for fish and shellfish that in turn attract raccoons and other wildlife who come to feed. You may see a gourmet diner or two if you walk quietly and keep your eyes open.

As you near the end of the park road, you will pass **Mzarek Pond**, another lovely birdwatching spot, especially rewarding during the winter months. Roseate spoonbills often come to this quiet, glassy pond to feed, along with many other common and exotic waterfowl.

The road ends at the **Flamingo Visitor Center** (38 miles from the main entrance; 813-695-3101, ext. 182), where a remote fishing village once stood. Early settlers could reach the area only by boat, and all sorts of activity, legal and not, went on here. Along with fishing and farming and the making of charcoal, businesses at various times included production of moonshine whiskey and the gathering of bird plumes for ladies fashionwear. The town is gone now, replaced by a marina, concessions, a motel and cabins, and a shop and visitor center. At Flamingo you can select from a variety of sightseeing opportunities, such as ranger-guided walks, wilderness canoe trips, tram rides, campfire programs and hands-on activities. Offerings vary with the seasons; check at the visitor center for a schedule.

Sightseeing by boat is particularly enjoyable. Most boat tours in this region, including some backcountry explorations, are available year-round. Sunset cruises are a delight, offering views of spectacular skies as well as allowing close-ups of a wide variety of birds winging their way to shore. In winter, pelicans ride the gentle waves, and gulls soar up and around the boat. Some boat trips will take you to **Cape Sable (★)**, the farthest-out point of southwestern Florida, where the Gulf of Mexico laps a broad, sandy beach.

For more birdwatching, especially in winter, take a short stroll from the visitor center to nearby **Eco Pond**. At dusk you may see ibis, egrets and other water birds winging in for the night to nest in nearby trees.

(For information on exploring other regions of the park's main visitor area, see "Main Visitor Area Trails" and "Canoe Trails" in this chapter.)

MAIN VISITOR AREA HOTELS

With the exception of Flamingo Lodge at the end of the park road in Everglades National Park, lodging can be found only in Homestead or Florida City. The usual chain motels line Route 1. If you are looking for less expensive lodging, head into the downtown areas of these twin towns, where you'll find rows of mom-and-pop motels along Krome Avenue. Some, like the **Budget Motor Inn** (1202 North Krome Avenue, Florida City; 305-245-0311) offer plain but clean and roomy accommodations and proximity to restaurants. Coconut palms and other tropical plants set this one somewhat apart. Budget to moderate.

A good place to stay and convenient to the eastern edge of Everglades National Park is the **Park Royal Inn** (100 Route 1, Florida City; 305-247-3200), an attractive gray motel with white trim whose 160 rooms are pretty generic but very neat and clean and carpeted. There is a heated pool. Moderate.

Despite the hokey stenciled signs tacked to posts, **Grandma Newton's Bed & Breakfast** (★) (40 Northwest Fifth Avenue, Florida City; 305-247-4413) remains pretty hidden to the average traveler, but it's worth finding just to meet Grandma Newton. She is a real grandma, and her tin-roofed frame house with beaded walls and ceilings and a big yard feels like a real old-fashioned Florida dwelling. The five pleasant bedrooms are furnished in what Grandma calls "mostly country junk," and the breakfasts of grits, eggs, meats, potatoes and fresh-baked biscuits make you wish you could visit every weekend. Budget to moderate.

To really experience the Everglades, stay at least a couple of nights in the **Flamingo Lodge** (Flamingo; 813-695-3101). This, the only accommodation in the park, is a plain old motel with window air conditioners and jalousies that can be opened to let in the intriguing watery smells of the 'glades and the shallow bay. Far from city lights and surrounded by jungle sounds, Flamingo Lodge lies in the heart of the Everglades. It offers a beautiful pool circled by tropical plants. Flamingo also offers rustic cottages with fully equipped kitchens and all motel amenities. Deluxe.

MAIN VISITOR AREA RESTAURANTS

There is only one restaurant in Everglades National Park, but there are plenty of fast-food chains and a variety of other eating places in Homestead and Florida City.

If you wonder what happens to all those good vegetables that grow around Homestead, you'll find bunches of them in hefty servings at **Potlikker** (591 Washington Avenue, Homestead; 305-248-0835). A barbecue pit smokes away out in front, preparing succulent ribs that are part of the down-home southern assortment of items such as pot roast, chicken pot pie and Cajun breaded catfish. The place boasts at least 11 vegetables daily, ranging from mustard greens to okra and tomatoes. The frame country-style building and mostly budget prices make this a friendly family-type eatery.

Martha's Vineyard (1235 North Krome Avenue, Homestead; 305-246-2002) is housed in a pretty little pink stucco 1930s-era Florida house with a tin roof and a lavender-awninged porch. The deluxe-priced menu is mostly seafood, grilled or sautéed in wine with special touches. There are also a few veal, chicken and beef selections. Apéritifs, good fresh vegetables and elegant desserts set this place apart, and the restorers had the wisdom to leave the lovely oak and Dade County pine floors uncovered for diners to admire.

Two doors in a low stone building lead to very different restaurants, both popular with locals. One opens into the **Capri Dining Room** (935 North Krome Avenue, Homestead; 305-247-1544) and confirms the marvelous aroma that wafts across the parking lot, for the budget to moderate menu here features pizza, spaghetti and some excellent Italian veal dishes. Try the other door and you will be in **King Richards Room**. Here the special is surf and turf, with broiled lobster tail and *petit* filet mignon. The veal is fancier here, and there are steaks, seafood and a fine wine list, at moderate to deluxe prices.

It's amazing to think that a scalloped awning, some pretty lace curtains and a few prints of Paris scenes could turn a storefront strip center unit into a charming French restaurant, but that's just what has been done at **Le Kir** (1532 Northeast 8th Street, Homestead; 305-247-6414). Such specialties as *médaillon de veau à la crème* and duck with grand marnier sauce contribute to the authenticity. Deluxe.

The handsome old building housing the **Anderson Inn** (★) at Anderson's Corner (15700 Southwest 232nd Street, Miami, just north of Homestead; 305-246-4400) was built in 1911 by two shipwrights and has served through the decades as a general store, feed store, rooming house and apartments. Now a fully restored historical landmark, the Anderson Inn is an elegant continental restaurant decorated with rich wainscoting and colonial wallpapers and furnished to look like an old country inn. Menu specialties include Flemish pepper steak with brandy cream sauce and veal Oscar with hollandaise. The spirits and wine list is extensive; there is a piano bar on weekends. Moderate to deluxe.

Although it's the only place to dine in Everglades National Park, the **Flamingo Lodge Restaurant** (Flamingo; 813-695-3101) is surprisingly good. The small but satisfactory menu features lots of fresh seafood along with chicken and beef. Located on the second floor of a small complex, the multilevel restaurant presents pretty views of Florida Bay. Tropical plants within and the dark night without remind you that, while the moderate menu is routine, the setting is quite exotic.

MAIN VISITOR AREA SHOPPING

Cauley Square (22400 Route 1; 305-258-3543) has a Miami address, but Homestead claims it, too. This restored area of historic homes and buildings encompasses a variety of shops, including a tea room, craft stores, clothing boutiques and antique shops.

The **Redland Gourmet & Fruit Store** is located on the grounds of the Preston B. Bird & Mary Heinlein Fruit & Spice Park (24801 Southwest

187th Avenue, Homestead; 305-247-5727; see "Main Visitor Area" in this chapter). Here you can browse among shelves of imported and domestic dried and canned exotic fruits, unusual spices and seeds, and out-of-the-ordinary juices, jellies and jams. There is a good selection of cookbooks and reference books on tropical fruits.

The **Knaus Berry Farm** (15980 Southwest 248th Street, Homestead; 305-247-0668) is owned and operated by a family of German Baptists who wear quaint clothing while running the marvelous bakery and waiting on customers. You can buy spectacular berries in season here, along with guava, strawberry and other homemade jams to eat on the mouth-watering breads.

On your drive to the main entrance of Everglades National Park, you'll pass a large, tacky, ramshackle produce stand known as **Robert Is Here** (19900 Southwest 344th Street, Homestead; 305-246-1592). Not only does Robert have fresh treats such as mangos, lychees, monstra, tamarind, star fruit and whatever citrus is in season, he serves up lime milkshakes and sells jellies and preserves "made by his own mother."

While the **Gift Shop at Flamingo Resort** (end of park road; 305-253-2241) has lots of the usual Florida souvenirs, they also have some interesting books on the Everglades, along with high-quality shirts and stationery.

MAIN VISITOR AREA NIGHTLIFE

From the Florida City/Homestead area it is less than an hour's drive to the bright lights of Miami and Miami Beach.

In Homestead and Florida City, there is an assortment of roadside taverns, and some of the motels keep their lounges open and provide occasional entertainment for late-night socializers, but most folks will tell you that the sidewalks roll up early around here.

If you spend any nights at Flamingo, deep in the Everglades, take time to walk outside (providing it's not mosquito season) away from the lights of the lodge and marina. On a moonless night, you'll experience a darkness that is ultimate and hear sounds made nowhere else in the United States, as the subtropical jungle creatures begin their night-long serenades.

MAIN VISITOR AREA BEACHES AND PARKS

Chekika State Recreation Area—This 640-acre park allows easy exploration of some of the many Everglades terrains, including a tropical hammock, tree islands and the grassy waters flowing over honeycombed limestone surface rock. The small campground is located in the hardwood hammock, providing a pleasant and protected wilderness experience within an easy drive of Miami. Alligators make their home in the park and are to be respected.

Facilities: Picnic area, restrooms, nature trail, boardwalk, interpretive center; groceries and restaurants in Homestead; information, 305-253-0950. *Camping:* Permitted. *Swimming:* Pleasant artesian-water swimming in a natural depression in the hammock.

Getting there: Off Southwest 237th Avenue in Homestead.

Biscayne National Park—This 181,500-acre marine park is the largest of its kind in the national park system, but most of it is hidden from the average traveler since it lies under the waters of Biscayne Bay and the Atlantic Ocean. The park includes a small area of mangrove shoreline, part of the bay, a line of narrow islands of the northern Florida Keys, and the northern part of John Pennekamp Coral Reef. Brown pelicans, little blue herons, snowy egrets and a few exotic fish can be seen by even the most casual stroller from the mainland jetty, but to fully appreciate the beauty of this unusual park you should take a glass-bottom boat tour or go snorkeling or scuba diving around the colorful reef. The little mangrove-fringed keys allow discovery of such tropical flora as gumbo-limbo trees, strangler fig and devil's potato. Birdlife abounds.

Facilities: Picnic areas, restrooms, nature trails, boat tours, boat rentals; information, 305-247-7275. *Camping:* Primitive camping permitted on Boca Chita Key and Elliott Key; prepare for mosquitoes. *Fishing:* Excellent saltwater fishing in open waters; prohibited in harbors. Lobster may be taken east of the islands in season. *Swimming:* Not recommended except on the tiny beaches of Elliott and Sands keys, where care must be taken to avoid sharp coral rock and spiny sea urchins.

Getting there: Park headquarters are located at Convoy Point, nine miles east of Homestead on North Canal Drive. The remainder of the park is accessible by boat from Convoy Point.

Homestead Bayfront Park—This is a next-door neighbor to the mainland part of Biscayne National Park (see above). It's a very popular spot enhanced by a small manmade beach, grassy areas and some shade offered by pines and palms. Entrance to the park is through a dense grove of mangroves, allowing a close look at these amazing island-building trees.

Facilities: Picnic areas, restrooms, showers, marina. *Camping:* Permitted. *Swimming:* Pleasant, off a small manmade beach.

Getting there: Follow signs at Biscayne National Park (see above).

Everglades National Park—With an area of about 2000 square miles, this protected section of Florida's Everglades covers the southwestern end of the state and a vast section of shallow Florida Bay dotted with tiny keys. The main visitor area, with its 38-mile park road running from the visitor center at the entrance to Flamingo at the tip of the state on Florida Bay, affords numerous opportunities to explore a wide variety of Everglades habitats, ecosystems, flora and fauna. Naturalists are available to offer advice on how best to explore the prairies, ponds, hammocks, inlets and bay. (See "Main Visitor Area" in this chapter.)

Facilities: Picnic areas, restrooms, restaurant, motel, cabins, grocery, marina, interpretive trails, boat tours, boat rentals, canoe rentals; information, 305-247-6211. *Camping:* Permitted. *Fishing:* Excellent in inland waters, especially for largemouth bass, and in coastal waters for snapper, redfish and trout. *Swimming:* Not recommended except on certain island locations accessible only by boat.

Getting there: Entrance off Route 9336, southwest of Homestead/ Florida City.

The Sporting Life

SPORTFISHING

Tarpon, snook, redfish and trout are the four most popular fish that charter captains will help you locate in the western Everglades and Ten Thousand Islands region. Contact one of the following for a fishing trip: **Rod and Gun Club** (Everglades City; 813-695-2101), **Captain Dan** (Chokoloskee; 813-695-4573), **Kingfisher Charters** (Chokoloskee; 813-695-4052) or **Island Charters** (Chokoloskee; 813-695-2286).

CANOEING

For canoe rental, outfitting and guided trips in the eastern Everglades, try **North American Canoe Tours** (Route 29, Everglades City, across from the National Park Ranger Station; 813-695-4666) or **Glades Haven Recreational Resort** (800 Southeast Copeland Avenue, Everglades City; 813-695-2746).

A limited number of canoes are allowed (and may be rented) each day for exploration of the **Collier-Seminole State Park** (Route 41, 20 miles northwest of Everglades City, 813-394-3397).

You can canoe the intriguing streams and ponds of the southern part of the Everglades through the **Flamingo Lodge Marina** (Flamingo; 305-243-2241).

HOUSEBOATING

To go houseboating in the southernmost Everglades and Florida Bay, contact **Flamingo Lodge** (Flamingo; 305-253-2241).

BICYCLING

You can bike the paved roads of the visitor areas in Everglades National Park; the only specific bikeway is the 15-mile loop road at Shark Valley, which is shared with hikers and the sightseeing tram.

BIKE RENTALS   Bicycles are for rent for exploring the **Shark Valley** day-use area of the Everglades National Park (Route 41, 35 miles west of Miami; 305-221-8455).

HIKING

TAMIAMI TRAIL AREA TRAILS   **Shark Valley Trail** (15 miles) in Everglades National Park leads hikers across a sawgrass waterway where they are sure to see alligators and a wide assortment of birds such as snail kites, wood storks and ibis. They may also observe deer, turtles, snakes and otter. Along the way is an observation tower that offers a good overview of the "river of grass." Because of lack of shade and few facilities along this paved walkway, only well-equipped, hearty hikers should attempt the entire 15-mile loop. Two short nature trails are located near the entrance to Shark Valley.

Big Cypress Trail South (27 miles) is a loop trail that begins at the Oasis Ranger Station on Route 41 west of Shark Valley. This wilderness trail, for experienced hikers only, plunges deep into the Big Cypress Swamp, which is actually a vast region of sandy pine islands, mixed hardwood hammocks, wet and dry prairies and mysterious marshes. Stunted bald cypress stand among the grasses; wildlife is abundant.

Collier-Seminole State Park Hiking Trail (6.5 miles) explores a section of the northwestern edge of the Florida Everglades. This low-lying trail winds through pine flatwoods and cypress swamps where one can observe a variety of plants and wildlife, including a number of endangered species.

MAIN VISITOR AREA TRAILS   **Elliott Key Nature Trail** (7 miles) in Biscayne National Park varies in difficulty as it follows the "spite highway" (a road bulldozed by developers in the 1960s in an effort to keep the island from becoming a part of the national park), a boardwalk, an interpretive nature trail and some undeveloped areas. The trail, alternately paralleling bay and ocean, crosses some interesting hardwood hammock jungles.

A number of **short interpretive trails**, .5 miles or less, are accessible in the main section of the Everglades National Park from the Park Road (Route 9336) between the main entrance and Flamingo. These short walks acquaint visitors with some of the varied flora, fauna and terrain of the huge park (see "Main Visitor Area" in this chapter).

Longer trails allow hikers to explore the coastal prairie and delve deeper into the mysteries of the Everglades. As they are sometimes under water, be sure to check at the ranger station or visitor center before starting out. These trails include the following:

Long Pine Key Trail (7 miles), beginning on the road to Long Pine Key, is a network of interconnecting trails running through an unusually diverse pineland forest. About 200 types of plants, including 30 found nowhere else on earth, grow here. Among the mammals spotted along the trail are white-tailed deer, opossums, raccoons and the seldom-seen, endangered Florida panther.

Snake Bight Trail (4 miles) commences about six miles northeast of Flamingo off the park road and heads due south to a boardwalk at Florida Bay. Three miles along, it is joined by **Rowdy Bend Trail** (5 miles). The two make a good loop hike through a variety of terrains and flora.

Alligator Creek Trail (14.6 miles) begins at the Snake Bight Canal Road and follows an old route used by pickers of wild cotton in the 1930s. The round-trip route passes through hardwood hammocks and coastal prairie to Alligator Creek. This is one of the more strenuous trails in the park.

Bear Lake Trail (4 miles) begins three miles northeast of Flamingo at the end of Bear Lake Road. This raised trail was made with fill dirt from the digging of the Homestead Canal and heads due west, skirting a canoe trail and the north shore of Bear Lake.

The **Christian Point Trail** (4 miles) begins about 1.5 miles northeast of Flamingo, travels across coastal prairie and winds through mangrove thickets to the shore of Florida Bay.

Coastal Prairie Trail (13 miles) follows an old roadbed leading to Cape Sable. This trail can be quite demanding, depending on ground conditions, as it progresses through open salt marsh and tends to flood. The trail begins at Flamingo and ends at Clubhouse Beach on the edge of Florida Bay.

CANOE TRAILS

TAMIAMI TRAIL AREA   **Wilderness Waterway** (88 miles) extends through a well-marked mangrove forest in the Ten Thousand Islands region of the national park. The entire trip can take from several days to a week. Backcountry permits are required, and arrangements must be made in advance for pickup and canoe transport.

MAIN VISITOR AREA   All canoe trails are accessible from the main park road. Check with rangers before you set out, as varying water levels may close portions of some trails in dry seasons. The park provides maps and guides for canoe trails.

Nine Mile Pond Trail (5.2 miles) crosses an open pond and travels through freshwater prairie. Though portions of the trail may be impassable in winter due to low water conditions, it is the best summer trail in the park, being relatively insect-free.

Noble Hammock Trail (3-mile loop) was once used by bootleggers, whose old "cutting" markers are still on the trees. This trail meanders across open country and small alligator ponds through buttonwood, red mangrove and sawgrass.

Hells Bay Trail (8 miles) travels through overgrown passageways of red mangrove and brackish water environments. A backcountry permit is recommended for this trip, even when not camping. There are campsites at the four- and eight-mile points.

West Lake Trail (8 miles) includes a long exposed crossing of the lake as well as a meandering trail through coastal lake country bordered by red and black mangrove and buttonwood trees and through the remains of a once-great living forest destroyed by hurricanes. Alligators and fish are numerous.

Cape Sable Trail (12 miles) begins north of the park road along the Buttonwood Canal and passes through dense mangrove/buttonwood regions into open flooded prairie where wading birds and ducks feed in winter. Several small lakes adjoin the trail; the last part skirts Florida Bay and is exposed, ending at the extensive beach at Cape Sable on the far southwestern tip of Florida's mainland.

Bear Lake Trail (5.5 miles) crosses shallow Mud Lake, which has a prairie, mangrove and buttonwood shoreline, making it good for birdwatching. The trip continues to Coot Bay through what may have once been a Calusa Indian canal and returns via the Buttonwood Canal.

Canoeing is also possible in **Florida Bay**, depending on wind and weather conditions. There is good birding in the shallows; during the dry months, the bay is the only realistic way to reach the beach at Cape Sable. But be sure to check with rangers on tides and weather conditions before setting out. It's a hefty jaunt to the beautiful but isolated sandy beach area, and sudden winds could make the return trip very difficult.

Transportation

BY CAR

From Miami, **Route 41**, the Tamiami Trail, heads due west through the middle of the Everglades, skirting the northern boundary of Everglades National Park. **Route 1** and the almost-parallel **Florida Turnpike** head toward Homestead and Florida City, where **Route 27** branches off into the heart of Everglades National Park.

BY AIR

Many visitors to the Everglades arrive via Miami. **Miami International Airport** (Wilcox Field) is a megaport served by numerous domestic/international carriers, including American Airlines, Continental Airlines, Delta Airlines, Eastern Airlines, Midway Airlines, Northwest Airlines, Pan American World Airways, Trans World Airlines, United Airlines and USAir.

There are even more international carriers: Aerolineas Argentinas, Aeromexico, AeroPeru, Air Canada, Air France, Air Jamaica, Air Panama, ALM-Antillean Airlines, Aviateca, Bahamasair, British Airways, BWIA International, Cayman Airways, Ecuatoriana Airlines, El Al Israel Airlines, Haiti Trans Air, LAB-Bolivia, Lanchile, Lufthansa, Mexicana, Royal Jordanian, Taca, Varig Brazilian Airlines, Viasa and Virgin Atlantic Airways.

BY BUS

Greyhound/Trailways Lines bring passengers from all over the country to the Miami area. The main Miami terminal is downtown at 99 Northeast 4th Street (800-237-8211). The Homestead terminal is at 5 Northeast 3rd Avenue (305-247-2040).

Astro Tours (2923 Northwest 7th Street; 305-643-6423) offers daily shuttles between Miami and New York, and **Omnibus La Cubana** (1101 Northwest 22nd Avenue; 305-541-1700) has daily service between Miami and Washington, D.C., New York and New Jersey.

BY TRAIN

Amtrak (Miami Station, 8303 Northwest 37th Avenue; 800-872-7245) will bring you into Miami from the northeastern states on its Silver Star or Silver Eagle. From the western United States, there are three trains to Miami by way of Chicago and Washington, D.C.

CAR RENTALS

Several major agencies can be found in the Miami airport terminal, including **Avis Rent A Car** (305-526-3005), **Budget Rent A Car** (305-871-3053), **Dollar Rent A Car** (305-887-6000), **Hertz Rent A Car** (305-871-0300) and **National Car Rental** (305-358-2334).

Companies offering free airport pickup in Miami are **Ajax Rent A Car** (305-871-5050), **Alamo Rent A Car** (305-633-6076), **Enterprise Rent A Car** (305-576-1300), **Express Rent A Car** (305-266-3266), **Payless Car Rental** (305-871-3540), **General Rent A Car** (305-871-3573), **Sears Rent A Car** (305-871-1444), **Snappy Car Rental** (305-884-8808), **Superior Rent A Car** (305-649-7012) and **Value Rent A Car** (305-871-6760).

THREE

The Keys

The Florida Keys are a narrow, gently curving chain of subtropical islands that mark the meeting of the Atlantic Ocean and the Gulf of Mexico off the tip of Florida. "Key" comes from the Spanish word *cayo*, meaning "small island," though it is said that the earliest explorers called this particular group *Los Mártires*, for the land appeared to them as a succession of suffering martyrs lying low on the horizon.

Until early in this century, the Keys were accessible only by boat. Isolated bits of jungly land, they attracted only the heartiest of adventurers and those who, for whatever legal or illegal reasons, desired to get away from civilization. The Keys' relatively brief history is dotted with pirates, salvagers, smugglers, struggling farmers and fisherfolk. In contrast, today these islands are easy to get to and represent one of the country's prime traveler destinations.

In 1912, developer Henry Flagler, spurred by dreams of carrying sportsmen to luxurious fishing camps and freight to ships sailing from Key West to Cuba and Central America, completed his greatest project, a railroad from Florida City to Key West. The remarkable line crossed three dozen islands over bridges spanning lengths from less than fifty feet to seven miles. The state's worst recorded hurricane destroyed the railroad in 1935, but its sturdy bridges and trestles became the links for the Overseas Highway, which would make these out-to-sea islands accessible to anyone who could drive, hike or bike the hundred-plus miles from the mainland to Key West.

Some of the Keys are so narrow that you can watch the sun rise over the Atlantic and see it set into the Gulf of Mexico just by strolling across the road. To the east of the chain lie the continental United States' only living coral reefs, popular with divers, snorkelers and passengers in glass-bottom boats. Because of these protective reefs, there is little surf, hence few sandy beaches in the Keys, a surprise to most visitors.

Time, folks claim, means little in the Keys. Visitors soon discover that slowing down is both easy and essential, especially if there's a traffic problem on the Overseas Highway (Route 1) or when the weather is too good to pass up, which it is most of the time. The Keys are basically vacation and retirement havens these days, now that wrecked sailing ships no longer yield up their booty on the rocky reefs, now that the sponge beds are gone and the commercial fishing industry has greatly dwindled. Romantics call these Keys "America's Caribbean Islands," "the islands you can drive to" and even "the last resort." Accommodations range from crowded RV and trailer parks to motels with a boat dock for each room to luxurious resorts. Dining runs the gamut from shrimp boils beside a dock to gourmet feasting in sedate restaurants. The basic fare, naturally, is seafood.

Fishing, boating and diving are the main sports of the Keys. Marinas lie on both sides of many of the islands; you can put out a rod for game fish from unused bridges as well as from classy yachts. Each of the centers of population claim to be "the best" of something, whether it be fishing, diving, relaxing, eating or partying.

Largest of all the islands, Key Largo is the gateway to the Keys and the beginning of the 113-mile journey to Key West. As Route 1 meanders out to sea, it passes through populated areas that could be anywhere in the country, with chain motels and restaurants, little shopping areas and ever-increasing development. But that's where the similarity ends, for this is a water-borne highway, heading into magnificent sunsets, bordered by sea or mangroves or marinas and even bits of surviving junglelike hammocks. Alongside it runs the vital viaduct, a huge pipe carrying water from the mainland. These dependent islands, though surrounded by the sea, once offered little but rainwater for drinking.

Closest Key to John Pennekamp Coral Reef State Park, Key Largo is the premier diving site of the Keys. Less than 20 miles farther along, Islamorada, on Upper Matecumbe Key, is centerpiece of a group known as the "purple isles," thanks to an explorer who probably named them for the violet sea snails that thrived there. The region is famous for sportfishing and was once the prosperous headquarters for wreckers. The next good-sized center of population is the town of Marathon on Vaca Key. The whole area is a popular winter resort and choice fishing spot.

Crossing the famous Seven Mile Bridge, Route 1 enters the Lower Keys, whose population center is Big Pine Key. The flora and fauna here are different from much of the rest of the Keys. Big Pine is home to the endangered tiny Key deer. One of the Keys' few fine beaches is found on nearby Bahia Honda Key. From here on, the population thins out considerably until Route 1 approaches Key West (presented in detail in Chapter

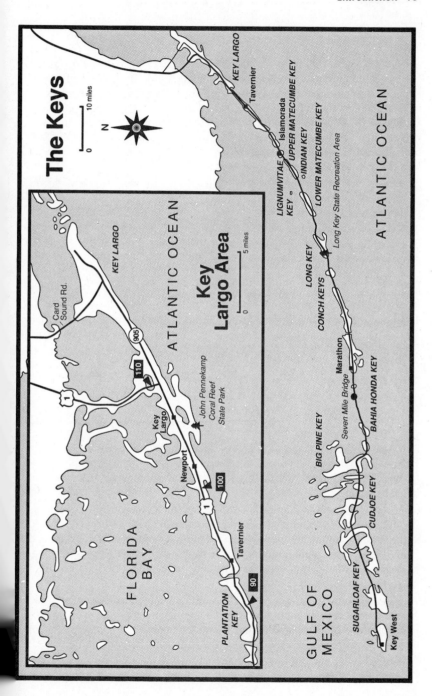

The Keys

N

0 10 miles

KEY LARGO
Tavernier
Islamorada
LIGNUMVITAE KEY
UPPER MATECUMBE KEY
INDIAN KEY
LOWER MATECUMBE KEY
Long Key State Recreation Area
LONG KEY
CONCH KEYS
Marathon
Seven Mile Bridge
BAHIA HONDA KEY
BIG PINE KEY
CUDJOE KEY
SUGARLOAF KEY
Key West

ATLANTIC OCEAN

GULF OF MEXICO

Key Largo Area

0 5 miles

KEY LARGO
Card Sound Rd.
905
110
1
John Pennekamp Coral Reef State Park
Key Largo
Newport
100
1
Tavernier
90
PLANTATION KEY

FLORIDA BAY

ATLANTIC OCEAN

Four), almost the outermost region of the state. Only the Dry Tortugas lie beyond.

One might suspect that the Keys, being such a narrow chain of islands with a single highway running through them, could not provide any "hidden" sites to explore. But they are there for the finding, little pockets of natural wilderness that have so far survived the encroaching civilization, small restaurants away from the highway, quiet lodgings on out-of-the-way islands, bits of history and treasure out to sea. Though winter is the chief tourist season in the Keys, breezes keep the days pleasant and the mosquitoes down most of the year. Rates are considerably lower in the summer.

So, if you are planning a trip to the Keys, get ready to slow down, to relax, to veer away from the fast-food chains along Route 1, to enjoy some sunsets, do a little fishing and find out what hidden pleasures the Keys have in store.

Throughout the text, hidden locales, remote regions and little-known spots are marked with a star (★).

Note: Mile markers, often called mile posts, can be seen each mile along Route 1 in the Keys. They appear on the right shoulder of the road as small green signs with white numbers, beginning with Mile Marker (MM) 126 just south of Florida City and ending at MM 0 in Key West. When asking for directions in the Keys, your answer will likely refer to a Mile Marker number. We use them throughout this chapter.

Key Largo

Key Largo is the first of the Keys you will reach by the great Overseas Highway, Route 1, when you leave Florida City and the mainland by automobile. The Spaniards named this "long island" appropriately, for it is the largest of the Keys.

Both the island and its main town are called "Key Largo," a name made famous by the spellbinding 1948 film about crime and a hurricane. You'll still hear a lot about the movie today, though its stars, Lauren Bacall and Humphrey Bogart, apparently never set foot on the island for the filming. However, a few local spots claim to have been featured briefly, and it does make for a nice piece of nostalgia.

The island's main thoroughfare, with its "any-strip-USA" fast-food ambience, tends to disappoint some visitors who had expected a more subtle tropical-island feeling. But there's also the overwhelming assortment of dive shops, which point to something that makes Key Largo unique indeed: just a few miles offshore lies the country's only living coral reef outside Hawaii. The jewel of Key Largo is the John Pennekamp Coral Reef State

Park, the only underwater state park in the continental United States. Here are facilities to introduce even the most confirmed landlubber to the sea kingdom and its living treasures.

Key Largo has a few other interesting sights, a couple of historic spots, plenty of shopping and eating opportunities and a wide variety of accommodations. Many visitors, especially city dwellers from Miami and environs, make Key Largo their sole Keys destination.

To get there, you can travel the busy, narrow Route 1, with its "crocodile crossing" warnings, or go via the slower Card Sound Road. The latter features a high toll bridge that affords good views of the mangrove swamps and a real feel for the early Keys, when fishermen lived in functional shacks and chain eateries were still to come.

Soon after arriving on the Key, you'll reach the hiking/biking path that begins at Mile Marker 106 and parallels Route 1 for about 20 miles. It ties in with a short nature trail, passes the John Pennekamp Coral Reef State Park, follows an old road to a county park and leads to some historic sites.

To find out more about these and other local sights, stop at the glossy pink shopping center housing the **Chamber of Commerce** (MM 103.4; 305-451-1414), which provides generous amounts of information on the Key Largo area.

Slow down as you approach the short bridge that crosses the **Marvin D. Adams Waterway** (MM 103), a manmade cut that creates a channel all the way across a narrow section of Key Largo. The banks on either side of the cut are the one place you can really get a good look at the geological makeup of the Upper Keys. There are fine examples of petrified stag horn coral, coral heads and other materials of the ancient coral reef on which the islands are built.

Whether or not you're a snorkeler or scuba diver, **John Pennekamp Coral Reef State Park** (Route 1, MM 102.5; 305-451-1202) offers many ways to enjoy this underwater treasure (see "Key Largo Area Beaches and Parks" in this chapter). An excellent visitor center features touch tanks, a giant reconstruction of a living patch reef in a circular aquarium, and other exhibits of the undersea world, mangrove swamps and hardwood hammocks. Glass-bottom boat tours, as well as scuba and snorkeling tours, are offered daily (305-451-1621).

Hidden under the Atlantic waters, the **Christ of the Deep (★)** statue is a favorite destination of divers in the state park. This nine-foot-high bronze statue was created by an Italian sculptor and given to the Underwater Society of America by the Florida Board of Historic Memorials. A duplicate of *Christ of the Abysses* in the Mediterranean Sea near Genoa, its uplifted arms are designed to be a welcome to "all who lived for the sea and who, in the name of the sea they so dearly loved, found their eternal peace."

Glass-bottom boat cruises to the reef are also available on the **Key Largo Princess** (MM 100, Holiday Inn docks; 305-451-4655). Choose from daily public cruises and luncheon, sunset and cocktail cruises with underwater lights.

If you want a very small bit of nostalgia, you can usually see the original **African Queen**, the little boat in which Humphrey Bogart and Katharine Hepburn battled the jungle and found romance in their 1951 movie, on display at the Holiday Inn docks (MM 100). If the ship's gone for the day, you can have a look at the *Thayer IV*, the boat seen in the Hepburn film *On Golden Pond*.

Atlantic bottle-nosed dolphins can often be spotted swimming and cavorting in Key Largo area waters, especially on the bay side. For a closer experience with these delightful and intelligent sea mammals, make an appointment to visit **Dolphins Plus** (MM 100; 305-451-1993; admission), one of several places in the Keys where you can swim with dolphins. Basically a research center, Dolphins Plus studies how these sea creatures relate to human beings and is researching the dolphin's role in "zoo-therapy" with handicapped and disabled individuals.

The little town of **Tavernier** (around MM 92) boasts a bit of history that local folks are hanging onto as best they can. Along with the Old Methodist Church on Route 1, a few **old frame houses (★)** with big shutters for protection against hurricanes remain, mementoes of the farming days before pizza parlors and gas stations. You can see them if you wander the few side streets and peer among the dense tropical trees.

For Everglades airboat rides and sightseeing tours of the Florida Bay backcountry (as well as fishing, hunting and nighttime frogging trips), contact **Captain Ray Cramer** (305-852-5339), said to be one of the best authorities on the region, an excellent guide and spinner of regional tales. He operates out of his home and will make arrangements to meet you.

KEY LARGO HOTELS

Many hotels and motels here offer accommodations that include dive packages, glass-bottom boat trips and fishing charters.

Jules Undersea Lodge (★) (51 Shoreline Drive, near MM 103.5; 305-451-2353) is so hidden that you can't even see it when you get there—because it's 22 feet below the surface of a tropical lagoon. You don't have to be a scuba diver to get into your ultra-deluxe air-conditioned quarters (there are two rooms for guests and an entertainment room); the staff will give you lessons. The reward is a unique underwater experience, with fish swimming by your 42-inch windows, no noise except the comforting reminder of the air support system, and the knowledge that you are staying in a one-of-a-kind lodging.

Tropical trees, dense foliage, ibis in the yard and a nice little bayside beach reinforce **Largo Lodge's** (MM 101.5; 305-451-0424) claim that "paradise can be reasonable." The price is actually deluxe, but for it you get one of six very nice, roomy units with a kitchen, living room and big screened porch with space for lots of diving gear. The place is beautifully maintained, and the owner is delightful. Do ask for a unit away from busy Route 1.

Marina del Mar Resort (MM 100; 305-451-4107) is one of those places with everything—lodging, water sports, marina, restaurant and nightclub, tennis courts, fitness center, pool and diving services. On the ocean side of the island, it is convenient to the popular nearby diving waters. The units are spacious and airy with tile floors and whirlpool tubs; there are also suites with full kitchens. Deluxe to ultra-deluxe.

The **Sunset Cove Motel** (south of MM 100; 305-451-0705) is really a complex of small, old-time, plain but neat apartments. This modest spot has a real old Keys feel. It's set among life-sized carved panthers and pelicans and enhanced with talking parrots and wonderful, relaxing Jamaican swings in the shade of thatched "chickees." The hosts obviously love being here and treat their guests to occasional jukebox parties and free use of their glass-bottom paddleboat and other small craft. You can help with the feeding of their friendly flock of pelicans, many of whom have been restored to health from fishhook wounds and other injuries. Moderate to deluxe.

Select from motel rooms with refrigerators, efficiencies or fully equipped apartments at the modest and clean **Bay Harbor Lodge** (MM 97.5; 305-852-5695). Shaded by palms, poincianas and frangipani, this moderately priced lodging offers a small, swimmable sandy beach on Florida Bay and free use of the dock and its boats.

At the **Stone Ledge Lodge** (MM 95-96; 305-852-8114) you'll have access to a nice dock, a small bayside beach, a shady yard and a pleasant motel room, efficiency or studio apartment in the long, low cream-colored stucco building. Typical of many of the area's mom-and-pop motels, this one is quite pleasant. Ask for a unit away from the highway. Moderate.

KEY LARGO RESTAURANTS

You'll meet both locals and returning divers at the **Captain's Cabin** (★) (45 Garden Cove Drive, oceanside off MM 106.5; 305-451-2720), a not-too-classy fast-seafood spot decorated with turtle shells, a mounted shark and several displays of finds from historic wrecked vessels. Fare is mostly budget-priced baskets of well-fried fish, conch fritters, shrimp and such, enhanced by lots of draft and imported brews. There's a big fish fry every Wednesday night.

For a beautiful, wide-open, classy place to sample Sicilian treatments of local seafood, try the **Italian Fisherman** (MM 104; 305-451-4471). On nice days they throw open all the doors along a broad expanse of bay, but even if it's chilly you can see a fine sunset through the wide windows. The decor is a mass of white wicker and blue upholstery; outside the dining deck is shaded by tropical trees. The *linguine marechiaro* (an assortment of shrimp, scallops, clams and the day's fresh catch all cooked in a marinara or garlic butter sauce and served on a bed of linguine) is a popular favorite. Moderate to deluxe.

The Fish House (MM 102.4; 305-451-4665), a smaller version of an establishment in Islamorada, is a good place for an introduction to typical Keys fare. Conch chowder is "in the red," thick and just spicy enough to suit most palates. Other Keys standards include cracked conch, stone crab in season and the catch-of-the-day prepared at least ten different ways. The tiny lobby features a real fish market; decor includes a ceiling hung with nets and lighted with fish-type Christmas lights. Moderate to deluxe.

An intimate fine-dining restaurant is **Snook's Bayside Club** (★) (off Route 1, MM 99.5; 305-451-3847). Very popular with local folks, this deluxe establishment overlooking Florida Bay offers fine treatments of seafood and splendid sunsets. A tablecloth-and-crystal restaurant, Snook's is a nice change from the dozens of roadside fish places.

If you get tired of seafood or want a little down-home mainland food, stop at **Mrs. Mac's Kitchen** (MM 99; 305-451-3722). This shack-style eatery has about the best chili east of Texas and pita bread concoctions almost too fat to bite down on. "Mrs. Mac" is actually a guy named Jeff, who broils delicious steaks and features different theme specials (Italian, Mexican, meat, seafood, etc.) for dinner each night. The place is small, with more varieties of beers than seats, so it's noisy and fun. Budget.

KEY LARGO AREA SHOPPING

Key Largo is the main spot for Upper Keys shoppers, so there are shopping centers, groceries and all the functional kinds of stores you might need, as well as tacky souvenir and T-shirt shops.

There are dive shops all along the highway of Key Largo. One of the premier popular full-service shops is the dockside **Captain Slate's Atlantis Dive Center** (52 Garden Cove, off MM 106.5, Key Largo; 305-451-1325). You'll find masks, fins, weight belts, tanks, wet suits and so on for sale and for rent. There is also an assortment of nautical jewelry, T-shirts and swimwear. If you want an underwater wedding or would like to meet some dolphins at sea, Atlantis will arrange that, along with their standard assortment of reef trips.

A well-known underwater photographer offers all the necessary equipment, for sale or rent, for capturing your diving and snorkeling adventures on still or video film at **Stephen Frink Photographic** (MM 102.5, Key Largo; 305-451-3737). Give him three days notice and he'll instruct you in equipment use. Staff are also available to dive with you and document your experience. The shop also offers some diving supplies and a nice assortment of artful clothing with underwater motifs.

The Book Nook (MM 100, Waldorf Plaza, Key Largo; 305-451-1468) has a large selection of books about the area and Florida in general, as well as maps and charts for divers. They also keep a good selection of classics and have plenty of recent bestsellers to keep you occupied when you've had too much sun.

For shells and souvenirs of the roadside variety, stop at **Shell World** (MM 97.5, Key Largo; 305-852-8245), one of a number in a chain that does a booming business in lamps, T-shirts and all sorts of curiosities that say "Hi From Florida," while not necessarily being made in the state, or even in the United States. But if you are in the market for this kind of stuff, this is as good a place as any; it's neat and orderly, with plenty to choose from.

Several places in the Keys specialize in embossed and hand-painted handbags, some ready-made, many with nautical designs, and others done to suit your own special wishes. You can find them at the **Florida Keys Handbag Factory** (MM 91.5, Tavernier; 305-852-8690), where they also make hand-embossed and painted skirts.

Island Silver and Spice (MM 91.5 at Tavernier Towne Shopping Center, Tavernier; 305-852-9541) is a sort of department-gift store collage featuring such varied items as high-quality toys to gourmet coffees and used Rolex watches along with their stationery, swimsuits and trendy sportswear.

KEY LARGO NIGHTLIFE

Some of the larger hotels and resorts have nightly or weekend entertainment.

If you're willing to experience a raunchy sort of bikers' beach bar in exchange for some possible nostalgia, stop at the **Caribbean Club** (MM 104; 305-451-9970). It is claimed that some parts of the movie *Key Largo* were filmed here, and it just may be true. Even if it's not, the sunsets from the deck are terrific. The joint is open 24 hours a day.

Coconuts (MM 100 at Marina del Mar; 305-451-4107) is a waterfront spot with live Top-40 entertainment every night, island music on weekends and a reggae band at happy hour. Inside, the huge dancefloor has a classy light show and a fog machine; outside, you can enjoy a drink on the canopied deck overlooking a canal with boats. Cover.

(Text continued on page 82.)

Kingdoms Under the Sea

The unique wonders of the Keys and Everglades do not end at their shorelines. From the shallows of Biscayne Bay to the deeps at the brink of the Gulf Stream lies a vast underwater wilderness unlike any other natural region in the continental United States. Close in are vast carpets of sea grasses, birthplaces and nurseries for shrimp and fish and Florida spiny lobsters, temporary refuges for endangered manatees and sea turtles.

A few miles out lies the coral reef. Here divers can explore a beautiful, silent underwater world of brilliant colors and subdued hues, of curious shapes and vibrant darting creatures. In some places its long spiny fingers almost touch the sun-sparkling surface of the sea. In other regions twisting corridors lead to secret caves at depths almost beyond the reach of life.

The reef is actually a living kingdom made up of billions of little colonies of tiny animals called polyps that snare passing microorganisms with their tentacles. They live in small cups of limestone that they secrete around themselves. The unusual and varied shapes of these cups give them their names: elkhorn and staghorn coral, star coral and brain coral, lettuce, pilar and flower corals.

The coral castles with their exquisite sea gardens host many other sea creatures, such as snails, lobsters, mollusks, crabs, sea cucumbers, starfish, sand dollars and sponges. Around the walls, through the corridors and down the paths swim exotic fish, as many as 300 species of them. The corals grow very slowly, some less than an inch a year, as each new generation builds on the skeleton of its ancestors. Though sturdy in appearance, they are extremely fragile and can be destroyed by changes in water conditions and by careless divers and boaters. In the early Florida tourist days, huge sections of the reef were laid waste by entrepreneurs collecting sea-life novelties for eager souvenir shoppers. Coral was harvested with crowbars and cranes; the queen conch population, symbol and food source for early settlers, virtually disappeared.

Many sections of this exotic underwater world are now protected, with tough penalties for even minor assaults on the fragile environment.

Mooring buoys for divers and snorkelers have been placed in the most popular areas, to protect the reef from damaging anchors.

The northern end of the reef lies in **Biscayne National Park** (headquarters at Convoy Point, east of Homestead; 305-347-7275). East of Key Largo, **John Pennekamp Coral Reef State Park** (MM 102.5; 305-451-1202), in combination with the **Key Largo Coral Reef National Marine Sanctuary**, encompasses about 178 nautical square miles of reef and sea grass beds. Southwest of Big Pine Key, the **Looe Key National Marine Sanctuary** (headquarters at MM 30; 305-872-4039) covers a five-square-mile area of spectacular coral formations and exceptionally clear waters (for more information on the parks, see the area "Beaches and Parks" sections in this chapter). Reef formations continue down through the ocean to the Dry Tortugas (see "Fort Jefferson" in Chapter Four).

Visitors don't have to be adept scuba divers to explore the wonders and surprises of this underwater world. Even first-time snorkelers reap rich rewards, floating on the surface in the shallowest areas where colors are often brightest and sea life most spectacular. Professional dive shops equip snorkelers and divers and, along with various park headquarters, advise on prime locations, water conditions and transportation options. (It is usually recommended that you avoid charters that transport both snorkelers and scuba divers at the same time.) Underwater visibility averages 40 to 60 feet and may reach 100 feet or more in calm summer weather. Some coral formations rise to within a few feet of the surface.

If you want to catch a glimpse of the reef without getting wet at all, board one of the glass-bottom boats setting out from several locations throughout the Keys, or stop at the living reef exhibit at Pennekamp Park or the Key West Aquarium.

Another underwater attraction is the host of wrecked ships (some claim there are more than 500 of them) that met their fates on the reef in the days before lighthouses marked safe passage through the Florida Straits. Tales of lost treasure and the challenge of archeological discovery keep hopeful divers returning again and again.

Woody's (MM 82; 305-664-4335), a late-night restaurant and lounge with a raucous bar crowd and dancing to a live band specializing in "Southern rock," boasts popular pizza, blackjack, pool and other such frivolities. If you're only hungry, they offer take-out food until 3:30 a.m.

KEY LARGO AREA BEACHES AND PARKS

John Pennekamp Coral Reef State Park—This remarkable place is the first underwater state park in the United States. Together with the adjacent **Key Largo Coral Reef National Marine Sanctuary**, the park encompasses an area of about 178 nautical square miles, most of which lies out in the Atlantic Ocean north and east of Key Largo. Most visitors come to see the coral formations, sea grass beds and spectacular marine life of the reefs, either by scuba diving, snorkeling or taking a glass-bottom boat tour. The land section of the park acquaints visitors with mangrove swamps, a tropical hammock with many varieties of indigenous plant life, and numerous shore birds. An excellent visitor center, featuring an underwater marine life garden, a touch tank and other interpretive exhibits, allows even those who prefer staying on dry land to experience a bit of the underwater world.

Facilities: Visitor center, picnic areas, restrooms, bathhouse, showers, nature trail, snack bar, gift shop, dive shop, boat rental, marina, docks; information, 305-451-1202. *Camping:* Permitted. Private RV and tent campgrounds are nearby, including **Key Largo Kampground and Marina** (MM 101.5, Key Largo; 305-451-1431) and **Calusa Camp Resort** (MM 101; 305-451-0232), which tends to be cramped but offers functional places for divers to stay. *Fishing:* Both among the mangroves (for mangrove snapper, trout, sheepshead, snook) and in the Atlantic (for gamefish such as kingfish, mackerel, yellowtail). Tropical fish are protected. *Swimming:* Calm waters in three small swimming beaches.

Getting there: Entrance is located at MM 102.5 on Route 1, just north of Key Largo. Much of the park is accessible only by boat.

Harry Harris Park—This county facility is one of the few public parks in the area for spending a day beside the ocean. It is spacious, with broad grassy areas and scattered trees. The beach isn't much, but the water is clear and full of fish.

Facilities: Picnic areas, restrooms, playgrounds, boat ramps. *Swimming:* Possible, in clear water. *Fishing:* Off the jetties.

Getting there: Take Beach Road at MM 92.5 in Tavernier; it's about one mile to park.

Islamorada Area

Islamorada (pronounced *eye-lah-mor-ah-dah*) was named by Spanish explorers and means "purple isles," perhaps for the way the land appeared on the horizon, perhaps for the abundant violet snail shells or the brilliant flowering plants found there when the islands were wild.

The Islamorada area begins at Windley Key (MM 85) and runs through Long Key (below MM 68). The community of Islamorada, on Upper Matecumbe Key, is its center of population. The area's brief ventures have included shipbuilding, tropical fruit and vegetable farming, turtling, sponging and the immensely prosperous business of salvaging shipwrecks. Fishing has always been especially fine in this area, and today tourism is the chief enterprise here.

The town is a collection of businesses that provide local folk with essentials while inviting visitors to "stay here," "eat here," "party here," "buy here." Holiday Isle, a gigantic resort and entertainment complex, dominates Windley Key with the latest in youthful party hype.

All along Route 1 you'll see signs for boat rentals, diving cruises and fishing charters. For, as with so much of the Keys, much of what the area has to offer is out to sea.

This usually calm and beautiful sea was gathered up into a giant tidal wave on September 2, 1935 that swept away just about every living thing and manmade object in its wake, including a rescue train full of evacuees. A poignant stone memorial and the red caboose that houses the **Islamorada Chamber of Commerce** (MM 82; 305-664-4503) are reminders of the storm that also destroyed the remarkable "railroad that went to the sea."

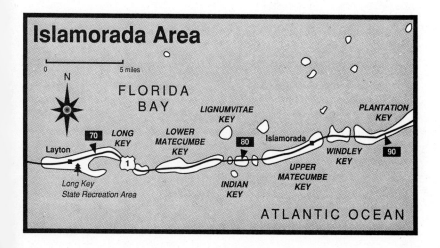

Several other sites, which can be explored on short boat trips, remind visitors that this Upper Keys region offers far more than meets the eye.

Among those trips, **Holiday Princess Cruises** (Holiday Isle Marina, MM 84.5; 305-664-2321) offers glass-bottom boat cruises to the coral reefs, as well as sunset and evening charters.

For a nice, friendly marine show where, if you're lucky, you might get to hold a hoop for a jumping dolphin or get a kiss from a seal, stop at **Theatre of the Sea** (MM 84.5, Islamorada; 305-664-2431; admission), one of the oldest marine parks in the world. It may now have fancier, more sophisticated competitors, but this place is still fun and quite personal. There are sea creatures that can be touched and fed, dolphins who join visitors for a "bottomless boat" trip and pretty tropical grounds to explore. Visitors can also swim with dolphins here.

Stop for a minute at the **Hurricane Monument** (MM 81.5, Islamorada) to meditate on the terrible storm of Labor Day 1935. Before the anemometer blew away, winds were recorded at 200 mph; the barometer fell to 26.35, one of the lowest pressures ever recorded in the Western Hemisphere. This slightly neglected but nevertheless moving monument was dedicated in 1937 to the memory of the 423 people who died in that storm.

You wouldn't expect a place called the **International Fishing Museum** (★) (MM 79.9, Islamorada; 305-664-2767; donations) to be a hidden destination, but this little place, next door to Bud N' Mary's big fishing marina, is easily overlooked. Established by a well-known area fishing guide, the museum offers small displays of old fishing gear from various regions of the country. It is also a museum with a message for people who fish: "Catch 'em, admire 'em, and release 'em," the motto for ecological efforts to preserve game fish. The folks here will tell and show you how to record your trophy without depleting the sea. There is also a collection of videos on the region.

The three-hour trip to **Indian Key State Historic Site** (★) (boat leaves from MM 78, Indian Key Fill between Upper and Lower Matecumbe Keys; 305-664-4815) presents the remarkable story of a ten-acre island that was once the prosperous seat of Dade County. Beneath the nearby, usually calm waters of the Atlantic lie the most treacherous reefs off the Florida coast, source of income first for Indians, and then for Americans who turned "salvaging" wrecked ships into profitable businesses. The bustling island town was destroyed in a grisly Indian attack in 1840. Today, rangers guide visitors down reconstructed village "streets" among the tall century plants and other tropical growth.

Another three-hour trip takes visitors to **Lignumvitae Key State Botanical Site** (★) (boat leaves from MM 78, Indian Key Fill between Upper and Lower Matecumbe Keys; 305-664-4815) and shows how an island was formed. This Key encompasses 280 acres; its virgin tropical forest is a reminder of how all the Keys probably appeared before people came in numbers. Ranger-guided walks through this rare environment introduce such unusual trees as the gumbo-limbo, mastic and poisonwood. The restored **Matheson House**, built in 1919, has survived hurricane and time; it demonstrates how island dwellers managed in the early days of Keys settlement, dependent on wind power, rainwater and food from the sea.

Near MM 66 lies the entrance to the **Layton Nature Trail** (★), an almost-hidden loop trail from highway to bay, winding through a dense hammock of carefully marked tropical plants, such as pigeon plum, wild coffee and gumbo-limbo, that are unique to the Keys. For travelers in a hurry, the 20-minute walk provides a good introduction to the flora that once covered most of the area.

Located 18 feet below the surface of the Atlantic Ocean, the **San Pedro Underwater Archaeological Preserve** (★) (1.3 nautical miles south of Indian Key; P.O. Box 776, Long Key 33001; 305-664-4815) welcomes divers, snorkelers and observers in glass-bottom boats. The *San Pedro* was a 287-ton, Dutch-built galleon in the New Spain fleet that left Havana harbor on a July day in 1733 and met its doom when hurricane winds drove it onto the reefs. The shipwreck park, dedicated in 1989, features an underwater nature trail where one can view varied populations of fish, crustaceans, mollusks and corals. Original anchors, ballast stones, bricks from the ship's galley and concrete cannon replicas enhance the park.

A **historical marker** west of Layton (near MM 66) marks the site of Long Key Fishing Club, established in 1906 by Henry Flagler's East Coast Hotel Company. One aim of the group was to stop the wholesale destruction of game fish in this mecca for saltwater anglers. The president of the club, which fell victim to the 1935 hurricane, was American author Zane Grey.

ISLAMORADA AREA HOTELS

The Islamorada business area includes another piece of Route 1 lined with mom-and-pop and various chain motels. If you prefer renting a home, condo or townhouse for a week, or even months, contact **Freewheeler Vacations** (Islamorada; 305-664-2075).

The most unusual thing about **Plantation Yacht Harbor Resort and Marina** (MM 87, Islamorada; 305-852-2381) is the open space that surrounds it, a rarity in most developed areas of the Keys. Here the 56 moderate to deluxe motel-style units are scattered across 57 acres of grassy open land, many with good views of Florida Bay. Units are not new, and some have fading wallpaper, but they are freshly painted, airy and clean. The resort includes a small, well-kept sandy beach with water clear enough for snorkeling, a freshwater pool, tennis courts, boat trips and rentals, and a restaurant and bar with live music.

Folks who enjoy being where the action is choose to stay at **Holiday Isle Resorts and Marina** (MM 84, Islamorada; 305-664-2321), a great complex of lodgings, swimming pools, bars, restaurants and shops strung out along a stretch of Atlantic beach. The five-story main hotel and its three-story neighbor offer oceanfront rooms, efficiencies, apartments and suites. Some are ordinary motel-type rooms; others are luxury apartments with kitchens, bars and wraparound balconies overlooking the ocean. Deluxe to ultra-deluxe.

If you want the glitz and fervor of Holiday Isle for lower rates, go a mile down the road to **Harbor Lights** (MM 85, Islamorada; 305-664-3611) for moderate motel rooms and deluxe-priced efficiencies. Owned by Holiday Isle, this place operates a free trolley to take guests to the bustling center of things.

The deluxe rooms and villas of **Chesapeake of Whale Harbor** (MM 83.5, Islamorada; 305-64-4662) have lots of cool gray and pink decor, appropriate wicker and other tropical-style furnishings, and access to grills, picnic tables and sunning-lounging areas. There is a small gesture of an ocean beach, a salt lagoon and a freshwater pool. The wide expanse of Atlantic for sunrise gazing is a real plus, as are the palms and Australian pines and the friendly white egrets and other seabirds.

At **The Islander Motel** (MM 82.1, Islamorada; 305-664-2031) you can snorkel in the clear ocean water off the fishing pier or swim in the freshwater and saltwater pools. The Islander offers pleasant hotel rooms (some with kitchenettes) and fully equipped villas with screened porches. The 25-acre oceanside resort is rich in tropical plants and features badminton, shuffleboard, ping pong and a restaurant. This is a popular place for families. Moderate.

Vacationers in search of sheer luxury have been coming to **Cheeca Lodge** (MM 82, Islamorada; 305-664-4651) for over half a century. Perched on the edge of the Atlantic Ocean, this four-story hotel has received a massive facelift. Much of the original wood remains in the updated lodge, which has classy lobby areas, spacious rooms, freshwater and saltwater pools, indoor and outdoor dining, a health spa, tennis courts and a small golf course. Villas are scattered around grounds shaded by a variety of tropical trees. A fine long pier invites fishing and serves as a take-off point for scuba divers and snorkelers. Ultra-deluxe.

If you are traveling with your boat, you'll like knowing about **Bud N' Mary's Fishing Marina** (MM 79.5; 305-664-2461), especially if you enjoy being in the middle of such sea-related activities as snorkeling, fishing and diving charters, party boats, glass-bottom boat tours, backcountry fishing trips and sunset and sightseeing tours. They have some moderate- to deluxe-priced accommodations for folks who love quick access to the sea and its offerings.

For moderate rates, you can stay at the quiet, unadorned, oldish **Game-fish Resort** (MM 75.5; 305-664-5568), which offers motel rooms, efficiency apartments or combinations for families needing suites. The place is very plain, with tropical plantings and a clear tidal salt pool complete with lobsters in the rocks. It's very popular with families and retired folk who like the quiet and easy access to fishing and who feel comfortable with the aging but neatly kept furnishings.

ISLAMORADA AREA RESTAURANTS

Folks keep coming back to **Craig's** (MM 90.5, Islamorada; 305-852-9424), an unadorned but appealing booth-filled eatery on Plantation Key. Especially popular are the Super Fish Sandwich, a full-meal budget item you can have either fried or broiled, and the Seafood Colin, shrimp and scallops sautéed in garlic butter with fresh mushrooms and tomato in a cream sauce. The pepper steak *au poivre* is far more than a pacifier for the non-seafood eater. Moderate to deluxe.

The restaurant with the reputation is **Marker 88** (MM 88, Islamorada; 305-852-9315), whose continental cuisine has rated raves from some of the nation's top culinary magazines. Entrées include fish du jour topped with tomato concassée, and rice colonial Bombay, a magic mélange of beef and veal slices, curry, shrimp, scallops, pineapple, banana, pimento and scallions. Nestled beside Florida Bay and shaded by waving palms, Marker 88 is informally elegant and intimate with a rich tropical ambience. The wine list is as impressive as the creative menu. Deluxe to ultra-deluxe.

Of the many places to eat at Holiday Isle Resort, the classiest is the **Horizon Restaurant** (MM 84, Islamorada; 305-664-2321) atop the five-story main hotel. You can get fine views of the bay and the ocean while enjoying Keys seafood prepared in a variety of fashions including traditional broiled or fried, and meunière or amandine styles. The chef also does a variety of things with Caribbean queen conch, an old-time Keys shellfish now protected locally. Deluxe.

You have two choices at the red-and-white-awninged **Coral Grill** (MM 83.5, Islamorada; 305-664-4803). You can gorge at the sumptuous, moderately priced buffet upstairs, which features country staples like ham with yams, fried fish and roast turkey, or you can stay downstairs and control your intake. Native fish are treated several ways; especially tasty is the "Matecumbe" style, sautéed with scallions, black olives, pimento, butter and lime. Except for all the sparkling lights in the trees out front, the place appears undistinguished, but the budget-to-moderate menu makes it good for families.

The shimmering mermaid on the wall of the **Lorelei** (MM 82, Islamorada; 305-664-4656) may catch your eye, but it's the trellises, ceiling fans and handblown light fixtures that give this yacht-basin restaurant a nice "early Keys" feel. They do all sorts of things with the catch-of-the-day here —broil, blacken, coconut-fry and serve it with Creole or meunière sauces. There are traditional conch chowder and fritters, too, and a devastating chocolate-chip Kahlua cheesecake for dessert. Moderate to deluxe.

Just before President George Bush was inaugurated in 1989, he went bonefishing in Islamorada and had dinner at Cheeca Lodge's **Atlantic's Edge Restaurant** (MM 82, Islamorada; 305-664-4651). The appetizer was stone-crab pie with scallions and tomatoes, a sublime sample of the excellent gourmet dining available in this elegant restaurant. Broiled grouper is prepared with garlic and black bean sauce, Florida lobster with béarnaise sauce and grilled baby vegetables, and chicken with sweet garlic and roasted eggplant. There is a fine wine list, too. Deluxe to ultra-deluxe.

Manny and Isa's Kitchen (MM 81.6, Islamorada; 305-664-5019) is a very delightful, very plain little place where chatter among the staff is Spanish and food is tops. A number of authentic Cuban dishes such as *picadillo* and *palomilla* steak with black beans and rice make a very ample budget meal. Regular Keys seafood and other American items extend into the moderate range. With 24 hours notice, Manny and Isa will prepare a special Spanish paella dinner for two or more.

The appearance of the **Mexican Cantina** (MM 81.5, Islamorada; 305-664-3721) isn't much, but the authentic aromas and wide assortment of Mexican dishes, including fajitas, chilaquiles and quesadillas, all accommodatingly explained on the menu, are a nice change from traditional sea fare. There are some interesting attempts at combining Mexican and Keys cuisine, however, such as shrimp enchiladas, fish Cozumel and the catch-of-the-day stuffed with crabmeat and guacamole and baked with cheeses and sour cream.

The Green Turtle Inn (MM 81, Islamorada; 305-664-9031) has been around since 1947, serving conch and turtle chowders, shrimp steamed in beer, home-baked breads and alligator steak along with all sorts of traditional seafood dishes and prime rib. The walls are papered with photos, and hundreds of dollar bills hang above the bar. It's a noisy, slightly frantic place when full, which is often. Moderate to deluxe.

Sam's Paradise Cafe (MM 68.5, Islamorada; 305-664-4900) is a pink-and-green little place that deserves a medal for bravery for locating next door to another popular Italian eatery. Sam's small menu specializes in such olfactory-tantalizing items as red *bragiole*, rolled and braised beef stuffed with seasonings and served with red sauce, or *calamari marinare fra diavolo*, a squid entrée you can have spicy hot if you are up to it. If you can't make up your mind, try the "Three Muskateers," a multiple-item entrée. Moderate.

ISLAMORADA AREA SHOPPING

The **Rain Barrel** (MM 86.5, Islamorada, 305-852-3084) is a store full of top-quality crafts, and much more. Many of the craftspeople create their wares right in this tropical setting that resembles a village more than a store. There are potters, jewelers, leather workers, fine artists and a maker of incredible silk flowers.

For a wide assortment of hand-crafted pottery, park under the trees and browse through **Plantation Potters** (MM 86.5, behind Rain Barrel, Islamorada; 305-852-5976). Sometimes you can see the potters at work.

You can buy all sorts of beachwear, straw hats, funky T-shirts and souvenirs at the **Bimini Town Shops** alongside the docks at Holiday Isle Resorts (MM 85, Islamorada; 305-664-3611).

For trendy sporting goods and clothing, as well as fishing tackle that includes handmade rods, gaffs, flies and trolling lures and reels, stop at **H. T. Chittum & Co. General Mercantile** (MM 82.7, Islamorada; 305-664-4421).

If you don't plan to get all the way to Key West, stop at Islamorada's **Key West Aloe** (MM 82.5; 305-664-9269) for the complete line of aloe vera cosmetics and fragrances that are produced in the island factory and sold internationally.

The name **A to Z Beauty and Nutrition** (MM 82.5, Islamorada; 305-664-4030) tells only part of the story. Yes, they do have beauty and nutrition items; the A-to-Z part refers to a varied assortment that includes shell souvenirs, trinkets and books for children, devotional materials, natural health supplements, antique jewelry, classy T-shirts, hobby guides and a very good collection of books on South Florida and the Keys. "We meet community needs," they say, adding that they might even order a size 14 shoe if you need it.

The **Green Turtle Cannery and Seafood Market** (MM 81.5, Islamorada; 305-664-4918) sells both fresh seafood and an assortment of Keys canned items processed on site. You can take home, or have shipped, cans of conch, clam and turtle chowders, turtle consommé, New England fish chowder and lemon and lime pie fillings.

ISLAMORADA AREA NIGHTLIFE

There's live entertainment every night in the restaurant/lounge at **Plantation Yacht Harbor Resort** (MM 87, Islamorada; 305-852-2381), a pleasant spot overlooking Florida Bay. It's mostly mellow, sometimes country-western, sometimes classic rock, usually featuring a single performer but occasionally a top touring band.

Nightlife begins in the daytime at **Holiday Isles Resort** (MM 85, Is-lamorada; 305-664-3611) with a host of party areas sporting such names as Jaws Raw Bar, Bilge Bar and the World Famous Tiki Bar. Signs also point you to "Kokomo," a beach bar named after the fact for the Beach Boys' famous song. There's canned and live music to suit a variety of tastes throughout the days and nights. Up in **The Horizon Restaurant**, atop the five-story main hotel with fine views of the ocean, there's quieter live enter-tainment for listening and dancing.

Next to the "all-you-can-eat" restaurant at Whale Harbor, the **Dock-side Bar** (MM 83.5, Islamorada; 305-664-9888) features live country and country-rock music and a raw bar. Come early enough to watch the fishing boats come in. Some consider this place to be a mellow alternative to the area's late-night teen haunts.

You can enjoy a quiet drink in Cheeca Lodge's elegant **Light Tackle Lounge** (MM 82, Islamorada; 305-664-4651) to the accompaniment of live piano music during the week and a small band on weekends. There's good, old-fashioned dancing music of the 1930s and 1940s.

In 1960, Hurricane Donna blew what is now the **Cabaña Bar** (MM 82, Islamorada; 305-664-4656) out to sea. After it was towed back, the place became a mellow bayside lounge. Musicians perform reggae and easy lis-tening "sunset music" nightly.

ISLAMORADA AREA BEACHES AND PARKS

Long Key State Recreation Area—Like the Key on which it is lo-cated, this park is long and narrow, its shoreline of shallow flats, thin beach-es and mangrove lagoons all shaped by the usually gentle Atlantic waters. Mahogany, Jamaica dogwood, gumbo-limbo and other tropical trees in-habit the tangled hammocks that, along with the mangrove swamps, can be crossed on boardwalks and viewed from an observation tower. Even though the traffic of Route 1 is closer than you might wish, you can actually camp right next to the ocean, shaded by tall Australian pines.

Facilities: Picnic areas, restrooms, nature trail, showers, observation tower, groceries in nearby Layton; information, 305-664-4815. *Camping:* Permitted. *Fishing:* Excellent saltwater fishing adjacent to the park and in deep Gulf Stream waters of the Atlantic. *Swimming:* Good.

Getting there: Located on the ocean side of Route 1 at MM 67.5.

Marathon Area

Legend has it that a worker helping to construct the awe-inspiring Seven Mile Bridge was inadvertently responsible for naming Marathon. Overawed by the challenge of spanning seven miles of open sea, the man simply called the task a "marathon." The appellation stuck.

Until the Seven Mile Bridge project was actually completed, the railroad line stopped at the outer edge of Vaca Key, said to have been named for the cows that once grazed there. Railroad workers were the major citizens of early Marathon, and the terminal contributed to a thriving local economy. But when the bridge was completed, the port lost its importance and the railroad crews moved on. Marathon quieted down, peopled mainly by fishermen of both the commercial and sport varieties and folk attracted by the laid-back life.

But Marathon is quiet no more. With almost 10,000 residents, it is the second largest city in the Keys, topped only by Key West. Tourism and fishing are the chief businesses here; there is seemingly not a species of southern sea creature that has not been caught in the surrounding waters. Retirement and long-term vacation living are popular, too. A number of small subdivisions have grown up around manmade canals that seemingly give everybody a "waterfront" lot and a place to dock a boat.

The Marathon area actually encompasses a collection of islands from the Conch Keys (below MM 65) to the beginning of the Seven Mile Bridge (MM 47) and includes far more than the bustling, traffic-filled, friendly metropolis and its occasional suburbs and resorts. Just before the outskirts of the city lies the oceanfront community of Key Colony Beach, a designed

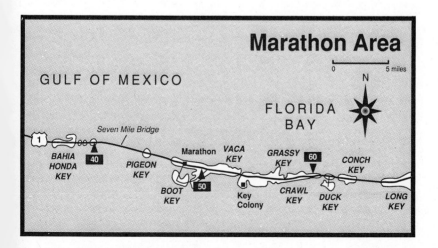

village where even the smallest houses seem to have their own individual boat docks. And here and there among these islands and from their bridges you'll encounter open spaces and fine views of the ocean and gulf.

One of those views hits visitors immediately upon entering the Marathon area via **Long Key bridge.** If you have not yet been overwhelmed by the realization that when you travel the Keys you're really heading out to sea, get ready. You'll certainly feel the impact after you leave Layton and cross the beautiful bridge over the point where the Atlantic Ocean meets the Gulf of Mexico between Long Key and the first little Conch Key. On most days, this meeting is calm and gentle. The horizon stretches blue on all sides as sea and sky meld. Travelers often stop at the little pull-offs on either end of this bridge—the second longest in the Keys—to take in the vastness of the water and the handsome bridge. Because the shore is sandy here, you will see people wading out in the shallow water or trying out their snorkeling and scuba gear.

After leaving the beautiful scenes at the Long Key bridge, Route 1 continues through several small Keys, including Duck Key, once site of a salt-making enterprise and now inhabited by showy homes and a large resort, Hawk's Cay. Nearby Grassy Key is home of the **Dolphin Research Center** (MM 59; 305-289-1121), where a tax-deductible contribution will allow you to play and swim with the friendly creatures. Your money goes, in part, to the center's program of providing rest and recreation for dolphins who have become stressed-out from long years of performance and the overcrowded conditions of captivity. (Like humans, dolphins can suffer ulcers and loss of appetite.)

Continuing on Route 1, you will encounter population pockets and empty spaces, skirt the residential and vacation village of Key Colony Beach, and arrive finally at Marathon, the last good-sized town before the famous Seven Mile Bridge. Stop at the **Greater Marathon Chamber of Commerce** (MM 48.5; 305-743-5417) for information on this bustling area, which boasts shopping malls, a modern airport, commercial boat yards and lots of facilities for travelers.

Hidden from the casual observer, though actually located in the heart of Marathon, is **Crane Point Hammock (★)** (headquarters of Florida Keys Land and Sea Trust, MM 50; 305-743-3900). Considered by many to be the most environmentally and historically significant piece of property in the Keys, this bayside 63-acre nature preserve of tropical hardwoods and mangrove wetlands contains many exotic tree specimens, archaeological sites and a historic conch-style house.

If you head toward the ocean at MM 47.5 (11th Street), you will end up around the **commercial fishing docks,** where you can watch the comings and goings of shrimp boats and other craft of the Marathon fleet.

To fully experience the Marathon area, take to the water. As well as the distinctive diving and snorkeling trips to the reef, several sightseeing cruises are offered by local captains. **Outland Charters** (Sombrero Marina, 35 Sombrero Boulevard, off MM 50; 305-743-7137; admission) offers trips around Boot Key Harbor and through some of the canals. Captain Earl Outland enlightens his passengers on the history, wildlife and exotic plants and flowers of the area and points out the visiting craft in Boot Key Harbor. Families are welcome.

For reef trips and sunset/champagne cruises, speed with the wind on Captain Fred Henn's **Key Lime Tri** (MM 54 at the Day's Inn Marina; 305-289-0222), an 18-foot sailing craft known as a trimaran.

MARATHON AREA HOTELS

If you like a resort where everything is at your fingertips, the 60-acre **Hawk's Cay Resort and Marina** (MM 61 at Duck Key; 305-743-7000) will fulfill your dreams. Here you can sleep in a spacious room decorated in salmon and teal and furnished with wickerwork rattan, dine in several very fine restaurants, bask beside the pool or on a pleasant manmade beach, play tennis and golf, or make arrangements with the concierge for charter fishing, diving or just about anything the Keys have to offer. The entire huge property is elegant but casual. Ultra-deluxe rates include a big gourmet breakfast buffet.

For moderate rates, you can have a basic motel room or a fully equipped efficiency at the **Valhalla Beach Resort Motel** (★) (near MM 57, Marathon; 305-289-0616) and feel as if you are on a private island with a quiet Atlantic inlet and waving palms. The dozen units are strictly basic, but the tiny beach, little boat docks and considerable distance from traffic make this a quiet and special place.

Several motels and small hotels line the narrow but pretty Atlantic beach at Key Colony Beach. The **Key Colony Beach Motel** (441 East Ocean Drive; 305-289-0411) offers small, carpeted, functional rooms for moderate prices, and you can dive into the large heated pool on those rare days when the ocean is too cold.

The **Ocean Beach Club** (351 Ocean Drive East; 305-289-0525) is a three-story affair with cool blue decor that suits its oceanside setting. Besides the deluxe rooms, there are apartments with fully furnished kitchens, a small pool and lots of beach chairs for sunbathing on the rare (for the Keys) strip of sand.

Route 1 on both sides of Marathon is lined with motels, hotels and "botels," the latter being places where you can tie up you boat just outside your lodging door. And you'll find that "resorts" can be anything from a small collection of cottages to a grand multiacre, full-service facility with a whole range of entertainments right on the grounds.

Sombrero Resort and Lighthouse Marina (19 Sombrero Boulevard, Marathon; 305-743-2250) offers bright, comfortable poolside and waterfront units ranging from moderately priced rooms to deluxe suites with kitchens. Everything about the place is appropriately light and tropical, from the sparkling pool to the breezy restaurant and cheerful lounge. There are tennis courts, a pro shop, sauna and 54-slip marina. Children are encouraged, making it a good family lodging.

If you're looking for a bed and breakfast, and they are scarce in the Keys, try the **Hopp-Inn Guest House** (★) (5 Man-O-War Drive, Marathon; 305-743-4118), situated in an oceanside home. For a moderate price you get one of three rooms with private bath and entrance, air-conditioning, views of the ocean, good breezes and a full breakfast. Owners Joe and Joan Hopp also offer several apartments, without breakfasts but with full kitchens, at deluxe rates. Papayas grow right outside the door.

If you're in search of unique lodging, you might consider the double-decker houseboats at **Boot Key Seaport Resort** (★) (1000 15th Street, Marathon; 305-743-4200). Securely moored, the boats are accessible from little private docks in a sheltered basin. These sedate blue-gray craft provide handsome quarters furnished formally enough for any ship's captain, and you can throw open the french doors to enjoy the comings and goings in the harbor. Deluxe.

Hidden Harbor Motel (MM 48.5, Marathon; 305-743-5376), typical of the dozens of moderately priced motels that line Route 1, has an added attraction—a large saltwater pool on the grounds devoted to an ongoing environmental project. Here you can observe large tropical fish and endangered turtles. A small marina and some rooms with kitchenettes also enhance the place, along with a freshwater pool for people, picnic facilities and some pretty coconut palms.

Reminiscent of old-time tourist cabins, **Conch Key Cottages** (★) (off Route 1 between MM 62 and 63; 305-289-1377) are located on their own tiny island accessible by a short causeway. This handful of rustic wooden cottages come in a variety of sizes; some have screened porches, and all are within easy access of a pleasant little beach. Best of all, they are away from busy Route 1. Moderate to deluxe.

Knights Key Inn (★) (MM 47, Marathon; 305-743-9963) is a two-story unit of older vacation apartments, almost hidden alongside a neighboring campground, where you can dock your boat for free. If your moderately priced efficiency is on the west side, you have a great view of the Seven Mile Bridge. Rooms are old-fashioned with a slightly nautical decor, and the whole place is somewhat submerged in lush tropical flora. There is a small picnic area; a few retirees stay here all winter.

MARATHON AREA RESTAURANTS

They call the **Caribbean Room** at Hawk's Cay (MM 61; 305-743-7000) a formal dining room, which makes it a Keys rarity, but it's not so formal that you and your family can't relax and enjoy it. The waiters and waitresses wear colorful Carib attire, and there's piped-in steel band music, but there are also soft, pink linen cloths and crystal, creating a nice ambience for enjoying the creative gourmet menu. Their seafood platter is a feast of broiled lobster tail and scallops, stuffed shrimp and grilled dolphin; the shrimp Caribbean is breaded with fresh coconut; for landlubbers the baked chicken breast Smithfield is topped with Virginia ham and cheese. Deluxe.

Taking advantage of a good Atlantic view, the airy **Beach House Restaurant** (399 East Ocean Drive, Key Colony Beach; 305-743-3939) offers dining outside or behind large expanses of glass. Royal blue glassware and white cloths create a nice ambience for partaking of anything from gourmet burgers to steak Madagascar with hearts of palm to lobster *fra diablo*, a medley of lobster, shrimp, clams and mussels in fresh herbs, garlic and tomato served with pasta. Moderate to deluxe.

Don Pedro (MM 53.5; 305-743-5247) demonstrates a creative use of a strip shopping center unit. Cuban cuisine is the feature of this sparkling blue-and-gray eatery located on an insignificant corner. All the entrées, such as *lechón asado* (roast pork), *boliche asado* (pot roast) and *picadillo* (a tasty hamburger dish), come with yellow rice, black beans, fried bananas and crispy Cuban bread. The very filling budget meals may be accompanied by tropical milkshakes or steamy, thick Cuban coffee and topped off with a dessert of flan, a traditional baked custard.

Brian's in Paradise (MM 52; 305-743-3183) has a menu with 12 large pages featuring humorous illustrations of Keys wildlife and something to eat for everyone. The emphasis is on seafood, the most popular item being the "Marathon meal" that provides a good way to sample local favorites— conch chowder, conch fritters, fried shrimp and Key lime pie. There are plenty of budget entrées as well as moderate selections, including the spit-roasted chicken entrée appealingly named "Bird of Paradise." The wide variety of sandwiches and breakfasts are served all day.

Search diligently for **Little Bavaria** (★) (MM 50, Gulfside Village Shopping Center, Marathon; 305-743-4833) and you'll be rewarded with a very authentic German meal of wienerschnitzel, pork *haxen* or bratwurst. Or try the Hungarian Rapsodi, a pork filet prepared with fruit and rice. The ordinary store space has been transformed into a charming European café with dainty lace curtains, a menu in German and English, a wide selection of imported German wine and beer and charming decor in white and Delft blue. Budget to moderate.

The art deco menu plus the comical cartoons of fictional chefs beaming at you from the walls hint that **Chef's** (Sombrero Resort, 19 Sombrero Boulevard, Marathon; 305-743-4108) is probably a fun place to eat. The small but well-balanced menu offers some elegant beef, seafood and chicken entrées; specialties include such delights as Lobster Sombrero (sautéed with artichokes and mushrooms and served on pasta with a sauce of garlic, wine and cream) or an appealing vegetarian *bouquetière*. The fish du jour is prepared five different ways, including blackened and baked with a pecan butter topping. There is an open grill and a glassed-in dining area alongside the tennis courts. Deluxe.

The lighthouse that distinguishes Faro Blanco Resort is authentic, and so is the fine dining at the resort's restaurant, **Kelsey's** (MM 48.3, Marathon; 305-743-9018). Along with creative treatments of local seafood, such as the seafood potpourri Faro Blanco clambake, this sedately casual place prepares roast Long Island duckling, veal shadows française with mushrooms and shrimp, and other continental gourmet dishes. The restaurant is lush with greenery, and its windows overlook the marina. Deluxe to ultra-deluxe.

Shuckers Raw Bar & Grill (★) (1415 15th Street, Marathon; 305-743-8686) seems more like New England than the Florida Keys. Outside there is a gingerbread trim and a tin roof with a widow's walk; inside, the open beamed ceiling is hung with old boats. The menu is informal and budget-priced, offering assorted fish baskets, barbecued shrimp and chef salads made with crabmeat, shrimp and chicken. At the raw bar you can get conch fritters, oysters Rockefeller and other shellfish that you'll swear just came off the boats pulled up at the restaurant's own dock.

Keep winding down 15th Street past where you think it ends and you'll come to **Castaway** (★) (turn toward ocean just below MM 48; 305-743-6247), a no-nonsense eatery on the working wharf where locals have been coming for several decades. There is a basic seafood menu with chicken and steak for the misguided, but the big come-on here is shrimp "steamed in beer—seconds on the house." They ply you with luscious hot buns dripping with honey even before you begin. Good variety of wines; moderate prices.

For a fine dinner in a simple but very pretty restaurant, go to **Bacchus by the Sea** (725 11th Street, Marathon; 305-743-6106). The moderate-to-deluxe-priced menu includes tempting seafood dishes such as "Catch of the Day Bacchus" prepared with tomato sauce, onion, wine and Bacchus' own blend of spices; other popular specials are roast duck, prime rib and lobster tails. For budget fare, try the broiled or fried shrimp baskets or mussels Provençal at the oversized outdoor Tiki Bar, located beside the working piers where you can admire the pelicans on the pilings and watch the shrimpers coming in after the day's work.

MARATHON AREA SHOPPING

You'll never have to go very far to find decorated T-shirts in the Keys; just about every shop has a selection. But if you go **Hooper Handprints** (★) (72 Coco Plum Drive, near MM 54; 305-743-4131) you can see how they are made. Prices are discounted here, and there's a good choice of these popular souvenirs, many designed by local artists.

Marine Jewelry (MM 54; 305-289-0628) manufactures gold and coral jewelry with nautical and sea-related themes, such as gold-capped shark teeth and gold Florida lobsters.

If you are looking for classy cosmetics and upscale women's clothing with name brands such as Calvin Klein, Rialto and Etcetera, you'll find them at **The Sandpiper** (MM 50; 305-743-3205).

Being the largest populated area in the Middle Keys, Marathon has several shopping plazas and all the basic stores needed for daily living, as well as the usual souvenir dens. For originally designed, hand-painted Florida Keys skirts and handbags, stop at the **Brown Pelican Store** (K-Mart Shopping Plaza, MM 50; 305-743-3849).

For a big selection of midrange warm-weather clothing and accessories for the family, try **The Knotical Shop** (below MM 50; 305-743-5322).

The Cake Box Bakery (below MM 50; 305-743-5809) makes just about every calorie-laden delicacy from bagels to birthday cakes, but the specialty here is "authentic" Key lime pie, which you can buy whole or by the piece.

Located in a big old warehouse, the **Village Market Basket** (140 49th Street, below MM 50; 305-743-6141) has rooms and corridors full of imported and exotic foods of all sorts. Stashed among bins and baskets of fresh fruits and vegetables, there are great jars of dried beans and spices, seasonal Florida delicacies such as alligator meat and boiled peanuts, and many other edibles you may have never seen before.

If you are doing your own cooking, or you'd just like to peruse the catches-of-the-day, explore the collection of **seafood markets** along the wharves at the end of 11th or 15th Street, on the oceanside near MM 48. These are outlets for some of the area's serious commercial fishing.

MARATHON AREA NIGHTLIFE

The Ship's Pub (MM 61, Duck Key; 305-743-7000) overlooks the water beside the showy marina at Hawk's Cay. There's live entertainment and late-night dancing to all kinds of music.

For live country-western singing and dancing interspersed with other entertainment, visit the lounge of the **Candlelight Restaurant** (700 Ocean Drive, Key Colony Beach; 305-743-0100). The four-sided bar makes for sociable fun.

Lots of locals drop in at **The Landing** (on causeway to Key Colony Beach, near MM 54; 305-743-0774) to hear the live music and enjoy a planter's punch or a Goombay smash. Usually there's a singer and a guitar with a little comedy thrown in; families eat here during earlier hours; it's that kind of friendly waterside spot.

The Quay (MM 54, Marathon; 305-289-1810) is so popular that it has clones in Key Largo and Key West. You can enjoy the sunsets, full meals and tropical drinks at this wicker-furnished, brightly decorated gulfside spot, where there's live entertainment every night.

Good Times (19 Sombrero Boulevard, Marathon; 305-743-4108), in the middle of Sombrero Resort, has a variety of live performers who play deep into the wee hours of the night. Tropical drinks are the specialty at this cheerful poolside place.

While **The Side Door** (just below MM 50; 305-743-4622) is mainly disco dancing and occasional live entertainment popular with the younger crowd, there's another dimension through a separate door—a cinema where you can drink and munch while enjoying a first-run film.

You can dance or play darts as local and imported bands play soft rock and other music nightly at **Angler's Lounge** (MM 48.3, Marathon; 305-743-9018) at Faro Blanco Resort. This second-story nightspot has windows all around and a wonderful view of the harbor and bay.

Several arts organizations are active in the Marathon area, sponsoring or producing concerts and plays from time to time. For information on what may be going on during your stay, contact the **Middle Keys Concert Association** (305-743-8867) and the **Marathon Community Theatre** (305-743-9368).

MARATHON AREA BEACHES AND PARKS

Sombrero Beach Park (★)—This free community park is mostly a generous windswept grassy area with a few palm trees and a long, narrow spit of sand along the ocean, offering one of the few public beaches around. Though not spectacular, it is a good place for some sun and relaxation and an ideal romping spot for children.

Facilities: Picnic areas, restrooms, playground. *Swimming:* Pleasant in usually clear, calm ocean water.

Getting there: Located on Sombrero Beach Road at MM 50 in Marathon.

The Lower Keys

The Lower Keys, which begin at MM 40 just below the Seven Mile Bridge and extend to around MM 5, are *different*. They are different in geological makeup, in flora and fauna and even in ambience and pace from the rest of the Keys. Geologically, their fossil coral base is layered with a limestone called oolite (for its egg-shaped granules). Some of the islands of the Lower Keys are forested with sturdy pine trees, others with tall tropical hardwoods where orchids and bromeliads thrive. A number of endangered species, including the unique Key deer, struggle for survival on these low-lying islands.

Big Pine Key is the largest of the islands and second in area only to Key Largo in the entire Keys. Wildlife refuges and shopping centers share this island, the former protecting much of the unique plant and animal life, the latter offering necessary services for the people who choose to live in what seems a quieter, lonelier region than those on either side.

The Lower Keys boast the best beach south of the mainland and access to a fine protected section of coral reef offshore in the Atlantic. Though there are pockets of development, from collections of little frame houses to assorted elegant residences, frenetic modernization seems to have been held at bay. With some unassuming screened-in eateries, scattered modest lodgings and significant protected wild areas, this region offers more chances to experience the "old Keys" than any other.

Perhaps the most impressive sight in the Lower Keys is its initial access, the magnificent **Seven Mile Bridge**, spanning the sea between Marathon and Sunshine Key. The bridge that carries the Overseas Highway today is the "new" bridge, built in 1982 to replace the terrifyingly narrow but equally impressive structure that parallels it on the gulf side. The old bridge, referred to as "the longest fishing pier in the world," crosses **Pigeon Key**, which you can't reach but can view from your lofty height above the sea. Once a railroad camp for Henry Flagler's crew, Pigeon Key is an important historic site; efforts are underway to preserve its natural state and historic old conch-style houses.

Unlike the Upper and Middle Keys, most of the Lower Keys seem to lie at right angles to the highway. Another example of their differing geology can be found on **Bahia Honda Key** (MM 37-38), which features some white sand beaches.

As you look across to the southern peninsula of Bahia Honda Key, you will see a magnificent section of the old **Flagler Bridge**, with the railroad trestle on one level and the automobile highway arching above it, a masterpiece of engineering for its day.

At MM 33 you arrive at Big Pine Key. Stop at the **Lower Keys Chamber of Commerce** (MM 31; 305-872-2411) for a lot of good information about this area. In character, Big Pine Key is quite different from that large Key to the north, Key Largo. Here are burgeoning subdivisions, good-sized shopping centers, freshwater sink holes formed in the oolitic rock foundation of the island, and pine trees. The contest between development and the wild is apparent.

Living in uneasy relationship with the ever-growing population of Big Pine Key are the Key deer, a miniature subspecies of white-tailed deer that grow to be only about two feet in height. In the 1940s, the population almost disappeared, inspiring the establishment of the 4383-acre **National Key Deer Refuge** (headquarters at western end of Watson Boulevard; 305-872-2239). Occasionally you can spot the world's tiniest deer in the wilderness areas of the refuge, especially in early morning or late afternoon, but be warned that there are heavy fines for feeding or harming these endangered, fragile animals.

Not far from the town of Big Pine lies a good-sized freshwater rock quarry pond called **Blue Hole** (★) (2.3 miles north of Route 1 on Key Deer Boulevard), the only one of its kind in the entire Keys. It is inhabited by several alligators, who often lie near the shore, as well as turtles and various wading birds and fish. The nearby **Pinewoods Nature Trail** meanders through a typical Big Pine Key habitat of palms and slash pine and skirts a unique hardwood hammock.

Marine biologist Stan Becker will take you on a one-of-a-kind **Canoeing Nature Tour** (★) (off Route 1 at MM 29; 305-872-2620) of the Big Pine region. You may explore buttonwood forests rich with bromeliads, observe rare birds and Key deer, see the effects of wildfire (which is essential for regrowth) and become acquainted with much of the unique Lower Keys fauna and flora you might miss without a knowledgeable guide.

Only reachable by boat, **Looe Key National Marine Sanctuary** (★) (6.7 nautical miles southwest of Big Pine Key; headquarters at MM 30; 305-872-4039) is an exceedingly popular diving site. The spectacular coral formations of this five-square-mile area and the exceptionally clear waters make it a delight even for novice snorkelers. Several wrecked ships also lie within the sanctuary, including the 1744 British frigate *H.M.S. Looe*.

Captain Buddy's Family Fun Trips (MM 28.5; 305-872-3572; admission) will take you out among the islands and exploring the reef by power boat. For a sailing exploration of the area, including sunset sails, you can contact **Sea Trove Sailing Trips** (off Route 1 at MM 21; 305-745-1064).

By now you have probably noticed that some of the telephone poles along the Overseas Highway seem to be topped with great untidy piles of sticks and twigs. These are **osprey nests**. If you look closely, you will occasionally see a bird with its young. Ospreys are regular residents of the

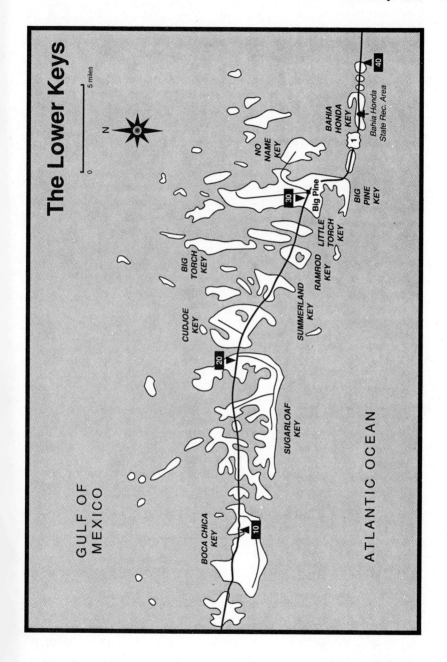

The Lower Keys

GULF OF MEXICO

NO NAME KEY

BIG TORCH KEY

CUDJOE KEY

SUMMERLAND KEY

RAMROD KEY

LITTLE TORCH KEY

Big Pine

BIG PINE KEY

BAHIA HONDA KEY

Bahia Honda State Rec. Area

SUGARLOAF KEY

BOCA CHICA KEY

ATLANTIC OCEAN

N

5 miles

0

Keys; some seem uninhibited by the cars and 18-wheelers that constantly whiz beneath them.

Higher in the sky, on the gulf side, floats a large, white, blimp-shaped radar balloon. This is **Fat Albert**, on the lookout for illegal drug traffickers and other interlopers. It is moored to a missile tracking station on Cudjoe Key.

If you take a detour toward the gulf on lower Sugarloaf Key, you'll get a glance at the **Perky Bat Tower** (★) (off Route 1 at MM 17). This Dade County pine curiosity was built in 1929 as the brainchild of Richter C. Perky, who hoped to get the menacing mosquito population under control by importing insect-devouring bats to take up residence in this louvered bat condo. Some say the bats never arrived, others that they came and, not satisfied with their carefully designed accommodations, took off for preferable climes. At any rate, the novel structure still stands and is on the National Register of Historic Places.

Heading toward Key West, you will see increasingly less development and more mangroves. Here and there you'll spot folks fishing off the old bridges. The densest residential area surrounds the Naval Air Base on Boca Chica Key. When you reach Stock Island, you have arrived in the suburbs of Key West.

LOWER KEYS HOTELS

Generic motels and small resorts appear here and there in the Lower Keys; rates are often lower than in nearby Key West. If you look hard, you'll also discover that some of the very best lodgings in this area are the hidden ones. If you'd like to rent a vacation home away from the highway, contact **Big Pine Vacation Rentals** (Route 1, Box 610-D, Big Pine Key; 305-872-9863). All the homes are on canals with boat dockage and fishing. Rates are moderate to deluxe; three-night minimum stay required.

There are three handsome duplex cabins on the gulf side of **Bahia Honda State Recreation Area** (MM 37; 305-872-2353). Though the cabins are not really hidden, because you can see them from the highway, many visitors are unaware that the six gray frame units on stilts are available for rental. Unit rates are deluxe, but the fully equipped lodgings with spacious decks can accommodate up to seven people. Make reservations by phone or in person, up to six months ahead.

For a moderate price, you can rent a completely furnished one bedroom ordinary little Florida-style apartment at the **G-Avenue Apartments/Motel** (★) (G Avenue, turn right off Third Street, which is near MM 31; 305-872-3395). No luxuries here, but they do have ceiling fans and access to their own boat dock.

There are only three bed and breakfasts in the Lower Keys, all really fine and, although neighbors, each distinctive:

The motto of **The Barnacle Bed and Breakfast (★)** (Long Beach Drive, one and a half miles from MM 33; 305-872-3298), "barefoot oceanfront living with panache," says it all. The owners, Vermont innkeepers for many years, built their elegant home in the shape of a six-pointed star, creating a collection of interestingly designed, distinctive rooms around a central screen-roofed atrium where gourmet breakfasts are served. Guests stay in either of two rooms with private baths in the main house or in one of the two efficiencies in a many-angled, beautifully equipped and furnished annex. Included is use of bikes, floats, snorkels, rubber boat and other oceanside paraphernalia. Deluxe.

Casa Grande (★) (Long Beach Drive, one and a half miles from MM 33; 305-872-2878), a Spanish-hacienda-style home, offers three handsomely furnished large rooms with private baths. A little shaded pavilion sits beside a small beach, hot tub, grill and picnic table. The varied gourmet breakfasts are served on a lovely screened patio. Deluxe.

Deer Run Bed and Breakfast (★) (Long Beach Drive, two miles from MM 33; 305-872-2800) offers two rooms, one moderate, one deluxe, with private baths in a very attractive Florida-style house with high ceilings, Bahama fans and good views of the ocean. A 52-foot verandah overlooks the sea and the natural grounds where raccoon and Key deer roam. The owner has cleverly decorated the outdoor area with driftwood and other jetsam deposited by the Atlantic currents onto the beach. Guests enjoy an outdoor hot tub and full American breakfasts.

If you'd like to stay near the area where the Key deer roam, contact **Canal Cottage (★)** (Big Pine Key; 305-872-3881). This quaint, natural-wood stilt home is so far off the beaten path that you'll have to ask for directions when you call to reserve for a two-night minimum stay. Depend on Bahama fans and breezes to keep you cool here; everything is furnished, including breakfast food.

The windswept, old-time one- and two-bedroom cottages at the **Old Wooden Bridge Fishing Camp (★)** (Bunta Risa at Bogie Channel, take Wilder Road at MM 30 and follow signs to No Name Key; 305-872-2241) are especially popular with anglers and divers who don't need a lot of amenities other than a comfortable, plain cabin, a full kitchen and access to the water. Rental boats are available, or stroll over to the Bogie Channel Bridge for some great fishing. Moderate.

The family that owns **Parmer's Place (★)** (at end of Barry Avenue, half mile toward bay from MM 28.5; 305-872-2157) has been adding more and more units to this attractive quiet collection of rooms, apartments and cottages for two decades. The result is an assortment of older and newer moderately priced, individually designed units, each named for an indigenous bird or animal and enhanced with picnic tables, grills, boat launch and palm trees. For a treat, request "Sail Fish," a large efficiency with a pretty porch right beside Pine Channel.

"Tropical paradise" is a worn out phrase, but it really fits **Little Palm Island (★)** (offshore at MM 28.5, Little Torch Key; 305-872-2524). This five-acre island of waving palms and green lawns features 14 luxurious two-suite villas, each one facing the water. For the ultra-deluxe rate you enjoy generous thatched-roof quarters with abundant windows, Latin decor, a private sundeck, meals in the excellent restaurant, transportation from Little Torch Key and enough quiet to calm the most jangled nerves. If you want to go fishing, touring nature preserves, diving or sightseeing, Little Palm will make the arrangements; but if you want to stay around, you can sail, windsurf, browse in the library, get a massage or just luxuriate on the island once enjoyed by Harry Truman and other notables.

There's nothing special about the moderately priced motel rooms at **Looe Key Reef Resort** (MM 27.5; Ramrod Key; 305-872- 2215), but it is very popular with divers, having a dive shop, boat ramps and dive trips to Looe Key Sanctuary available for guests. There is also a restaurant, lounge and swimming pool.

Sugarloaf Lodge (MM 17, Sugarloaf Key; 305-745-3211) is one of the "full service" resorts with average but pleasant motel rooms and efficiencies, most of them facing the water. Full service here means not only a pool, restaurant and lounge, but a three-times-a-day dolphin show by long-time resident Sugar, an air strip and seaplane rides, a marina, mini-golf and fishing charters. It's also very convenient to Key West. Deluxe.

LOWER KEYS RESTAURANTS

Island Jim's (MM 31.2; 305-872-2017) is one of many Lower Keys restaurants that make not one attempt at refinement but thrive on a good reputation. What is unusual about this one is that its fame for charbroiled steaks almost beats that for seafood. Perhaps it's due to the meat market next door. Locals start arriving around dawn for breakfast and eat at the counter or functional tables. Moderate to deluxe.

The **Cedar Inn Restaurant and Lounge** (MM 31; 305-872-4031) is plain but a little less so than some of the other popular Lower Keys eateries. In fact, this one is just fancy enough to have oysters with caviar and sour cream for an appetizer. Fresh fish is served broiled, fried, stuffed or florentine. They also have stuffed lobster in season and a 'gator appetizer that most people try just so they can say they have. Moderate to deluxe.

Though only open for breakfast and lunch, it's good to know about the **Dip N' Deli** (MM 31; 305-872-3030). (Like many other travelers on the way to Key West, you may just be passing through here in the middle of the day.) It's a nice place whose name tells all—there are fresh salads, 19 kinds of sandwiches, soups and lots of ice cream treats including old-fashioned sodas and milkshakes. There's also lots of local chatter going on here, as well as the refreshing break from the ever-present seafood.

Because it serves food from 6 a.m. to 4 a.m., the **Pelican Post** (MM 30; 305-872-3461) boasts four menus—breakfast, lunch, dinner and late-night. This unadorned roadside eatery is open to the elements and furnished with picnic tables. It's easy to imagine that visitors to the Keys in the old days found places just like it. Jambalaya is a specialty here, but the favorite is the "world famous fish sandwich," a full-meal item of grouper fried in tempura batter and topped with mushrooms, cheese and onions. Moderate.

To get away from it all in style, plan to dine at the restaurant on **Little Palm Island** (★) (offshore from Little Torch Key, MM 28.5; 305-872-2524). You have to call ahead for a reservation; they will tell you when the boat will pick you up to take you to the lovely, luxurious island resort. If you're wise, you'll go in time to watch the sunset while sipping a cocktail beside the sandy beach or partaking of the fish of the day, marinated sword-fish with *papaya coulis*, roast duck with fruit and vinegar sauce, or any of the other continental entrées. Deluxe.

Montes Restaurant & Fish Market (MM 25, Summerland Key; 305-745-3731) is a bare-bones place with plastic-covered round picnic tables and good old-fashioned fried seafood platters and baskets with french fries, cole slaw and sauce. Sit on the porch beside the canal and enjoy what you're supposed to eat in the Keys—conch chowder, conch salad, conch fritters, stone crabs and shrimp in beer. Moderate.

You can eat indoors or alongside Bow Channel beneath the silver but-tonwood trees at **Cousin Joe's Supper Club** (★) (Drost Drive off Route 1 at MM 21, Cudjoe Key; 305-745-1646). This modest, low-ceiling res-taurant features classic and Caribbean dishes. Specials include items like snapper Rangoon with exotic fruits, and conch, lightly breaded and sautéed with Key lime juice. Moderate to deluxe.

Mangrove Mama's (MM 20; 305-745-3030) is such an unlikely look-ing, side-of-the-road, banana-tree-surrounded eating establishment that you probably wouldn't stop unless someone recommended it—and plenty of Lower Keys folks do just that, with great enthusiasm. The floor is concrete, tablecloths are minimal, the chairs don't match and resident cats look long-ingly at your dinners. But the menu, though brief and to the point, is some-what fancier than you'd expect, with such treats as baked stuffed shrimp and chicken and scallop Caribbean, sautéed with bacon and served in a creamy dijon sauce. The herb teas and homemade rolls are as pleasant a surprise as the handsome brick fireplace, used on very rare chilly nights. Moderate.

(Text continued on page 108.)

Days of the Dolphins

As far back as the shadowy times of prehistory, man has been fascinated by dolphins. In Greek mythology, Apollo once took the form of a dolphin to lead a boat to Delphi. Various coastal communities around the world have greeted the dolphin as a bearer of good fortune, guider of lost ships, saver of human lives. Though scientists cannot interpret the actions of dolphins in terms of human emotions, it is easy to see why these lovely marine mammals have captivated the imagination for so many centuries.

Stand on a Florida beach and watch a herd of dolphins surface and dive, surface and dive again, or leap gracefully above the waves. The show almost seems designed for your benefit. Or sail into the Gulf of Mexico, accompanied by dolphins who dart in and out of your path, seemingly playing with you as you tack and turn. Though much of the dolphin's life remains a mystery, there is no question that they are highly intelligent and very friendly to humans.

Dolphins, like whales, are cetaceans. The greatest confusion, perhaps, comes from distinguishing dolphin from porpoise. To the casual observer, the most obvious physical difference is that most dolphins have a pronounced beak and a dorsal fin with a curvature toward the tail, while none of the porpoises has a discernible beak, and all but one have a triangular dorsal fin. Also, dolphins have cone-shaped teeth, while porpoise teeth are spade-shaped.

Another misconception that needs to be cleared up relates to seafood menus. Don't panic when you read "dolphin" among the special dinner entrees. This refers to a popular tropical game fish, not to the gentle mammal. It would make things easier if only restaurants would agree, once and for all, to stick to its other name, mahimahi.

Dolphins live a complex social life, often traveling in large herds broken down into family units called pods. Mothers keep an eye on their calves for up to five years, displaying deep affection throughout infancy. Researchers report that dolphins forced to live alone display unhappiness. Adolescents isolate themselves into groups of their own sex, not returning to socialize with the whole group until they become mature adults. No wonder we are tempted to think of them in human terms!

Yet however much we might like to identify with dolphins, and though their brains are similar in size to ours, dolphins possess many abilities that man can only envy. Most impressive is *echolocation*, use of a wonderful biological sonar that allows dolphins to locate food and interpret other objects, no matter how dark or murky the water, by sending out and echoing back their curious clicks and squeals and whistles. And unlike us, they can dive to great depths for long periods of time without developing painful, life-threatening bends. Located on the tops of their heads are the nostrils, remarkable blowholes with two internal passages, one for each lung.

Though fewer dolphins ply the waters surrounding South Florida than once swam here, sharp-eyed visitors can still reap their share of sightings in the wild. Besides, the Florida Keys have long been one of the centers for the study and training of these sea mammals. At the **Theatre of the Sea** (MM 84.5, Islamorada; 305-664-2431), one of the oldest marine parks in the world, you can watch dolphins do their hoop-jumping, tail-standing, fish-catching tricks. Several motels and resorts boast their own private dolphin pets who put on shows for or swim with their guests.

Swim with a dolphin? Yes, it is possible (for a handsome fee), and it can be a rewarding and, some say, almost mystical experience well worth the price. At the **Dolphin Research Center** (MM 59, Grassy Key; 305-289-1121), the income from your swim helps support an extensive program of therapy, teaching and research. Here sick and wounded dolphins are cared for, along with "stressed-out" performing dolphins who come to rest. You also can make a swim appointment at **Dolphins Plus** (MM 100, Key Largo; 305-451-1993), where research is being done to see if dolphins can break down the emotional barriers of human autism.

As interest in dolphins increases, critics of forced human-dolphin encounters express concern about possible harmful effects on these sensitive animals. Another group of folks has been boycotting tuna fish until laws are passed that will protect dolphins from tuna-netting practices that massacre thousands of the friendly mammals each year. The research centers will be delighted to share information on these subjects with you.

LOWER KEYS SHOPPING

For all the basic necessities, the main place for shopping in the Lower Keys is the **Big Pine Key Shopping Plaza** (on Key Deer Boulevard just off Route 1 at MM 30).

Edie's Hallmark Shop (Big Pine Key Shopping Plaza; 305-872-3935) is far more than it's name implies. Here you'll find works by local artists and an excellent book section with top-notch vacation reading as well as a good supply of Florida and Keys books and guides.

LOWER KEYS NIGHTLIFE

The **Cedar Inn Restaurant and Lounge** (MM 31; 305-872-4031) has live entertainment some nights and occasional special events such as sock hops and the like.

For an evening with the locals, drop in at the **No Name Pub** (★) (north end of Watson Boulevard, Big Pine Key; 305-872-9115), a funky, run-down eating and drinking establishment with a carved-up wooden bar, over 70 kinds of beer, darts, pool and a 1957 baseball machine. Sometimes they have bands, occasionally a pig roast and always the "best pizza in the known universe." This is a fun place that just about anybody can direct you to.

At the **Pelican Post** (MM 30; 305-872-3461) you can eat and drink until 4 a.m. from the special late-night menu. Sometimes there is live entertainment, depending on who's available in this neck of the woods.

On weekends there's live rock-and-roll performed by local bands at **Looe Key Reef Resort** (MM 27.5, Ramrod Key; 305-872-2215).

Pirate's Lounge (Sugar Loaf Lodge, MM 17, Sugar Loaf Key; 305-745-3211) is a typical resort-motel nightspot. This one has nightly entertainment and dancing, and boasts oversized piña coladas and strawberry daiquiris.

LOWER KEYS BEACHES AND PARKS

Little Duck Key Park—This little park on the ocean provides a place for a roadside rest and a swim just after you cross the Seven Mile Bridge, heading down the Keys. It's only a tiny strip of beach with a few windblown trees, but the beach is sandy, the swimming better than many places and the water usually clear enough for snorkeling.

Facilities: Picnic area, restrooms. *Swimming:* Good.

Getting there: On the ocean side of Route 1 at MM 40.

Bahia Honda State Recreation Area—This southernmost state recreation area offers what many consider the best swimming beaches in the

Keys—wider and leading into deeper water than most. Remnants of the un-developed Keys remain in this beautiful park—silver palms, satinwood, dwarf morning glories and a number of rare birds such as the roseate spoon-bill and white-crowned pigeon. You may camp in the wide open spaces (best choice during mosquito season) in view of a handsome segment of Henry Flagler's original old bridge, or in the shady hardwood hammock at Sand-spur Beach.

Facilities: Picnic areas, restrooms, cabins, bathhouse, nature trail, concession stand, marina, dive shop, limited groceries; information, 305-872-2353. *Camping:* Permitted. *Fishing:* Excellent, both in bay and ocean; guides available during tarpon season. *Swimming:* Excellent, both in the At-lantic Ocean and Gulf of Mexico.

Getting there: The entrance is located on the ocean side of Route 1 at MM 37.

The Sporting Life

SPORTFISHING

Visitors can go sportfishing on a pricey, custom-designed charter or by joining one of the numerous party boats on a scheduled trip.

For charter fishing in Biscayne Bay and the Atlantic Ocean in the vicin-ity of the Upper Keys, for such gamefish as amberjack, barracuda, bonefish, blackfin tuna and tarpon, contact **Club Biscayne Boat Rental Corporation** (2698 Southwest 328th Street, Homestead; 305-245-4020).

Charters and guides for fishing both the backcountry and ocean waters out of Key Largo can be had from **Back Country Adventures** (MM 105; 305-451-1247) or **Miss Kitty Reef Fishing** (MM 100; 305-451-2220), among many, many others.

In Islamorada, there are also dozens of sportfishing outfits to choose from, including **Dux Spray Charters** (MM 83.5; 305-664-5214) and **Win-ter Hawk Charters** (MM 73.5; 305-664-5567). **Holiday Isle Resorts & Marina** (MM 84; 305-664-2321) will make arrangements for both back-country and offshore fishing trips and charters.

In Marathon, charter booking services are offered by **The World Class Angler** (MM 48.3 at Faro Blanco Resort; 305-743-6139). **Marathon Lady Party Boats** (MM 53 at Vaca Cut; 305-743-5580) offers a variety of day and night fishing trips. For flats fishing join Captain Barry Meyer on the **Magic** (1000 15th Street; 305-743-3278).

In the Lower Keys, you can go backcountry, flats or offshore fishing with **Bogie Channel Charters** (MM 30, Big Pine Key; 305-872-9744). **Fan-

tasy Charters (MM 28, Big Pine Key; 305-872-3200) will take you offshore and to the reef. Try backcountry fishing on the **Outcast** (MM 77, Sugarloaf Key; 305-745-1503).

SKINDIVING

On any calm and beautiful day the sea to the east of Florida's Upper Keys is dotted with boats. They belong to the scuba divers and snorkelers who are captivated by the beauty of the continental United States' only living reef. Others search the remains of ships wrecked on that same lovely reef. Many communities in the Keys have dozens of scuba shops and dive centers designed to meet the needs of both novice snorkeler and sophisticated diver.

For scuba and snorkel trips via glass-bottom boat to the northern tip of the reef, contact the **Biscayne Aqua Center** (Convoy Point, end of Southwest 38th Street, east of Homestead; 305-247-2400) at the headquarters of the Biscayne National Park.

Route 1 in the Key Largo area seems like one continuous dive shop. To meet your diving needs, try **The Coral Reef Park Company** (John Pennekamp Coral Reef State Park, MM 102.5, Key Largo; 305-451-1621), **American Diving Headquarters** (MM 106; 305-451-0037) or **Divers' World** (MM 100; 305-451-3200). At Tavernier, try the **Florida Keys Dive Center** (MM 90.5; 305-852-4599).

Diving courses, gear and reef and wreck trips are available in Islamorada through **Lady Cyana Divers** (MM 85.9; 305-664-8717), **Buddy's Dive Shop** (MM 85; 305-664-4707) and **Holiday Isle Resorts & Marina** (MM 84; 305-664-2321).

In Marathon, contact **The Diving Site** (MM 53.5; 305-289-1021) or **Seaview Ocean Divers** (MM 50.5; 305-743-8514) for reef trips, lessons and equipment.

Looe Key Reef Resort (MM 27.5, Ramrod Key; 305-872-2215) and **Cudjoe Gardens Marina and Dive Shop** (MM 21, Cudjoe Key; 305-745-2357) are full-service dive centers in the Lower Keys.

BOATING

Boat rentals are available throughout the Keys. In Key Largo try **Jarmada Boat Rental** (MM 107; 305-451-2628) or **Conch Boat Rentals** (MM 100; 305-451-2220) or go on down to Tavernier to the **Tavernier Creek Boat Rentals** (MM 90.5; 305-852-5854). In Islamorada, you can arrange boat rentals through **Holiday Isle Resorts & Marina** (MM 84; 305-664-2321) or go to **Robbie's Boat Rentals** (MM 77.5; 305-664-4351). **Boat Rentals** at Poseidon Harbor (MM 63, Conch Key; 305-289-1525) rents power boats and a glass-bottom skiff, or go down through Marathon to **Clyde's 7 Mile Marina** (MM 47.5; 305-743-7712) for boat rentals and fishing guides. In the Lower Keys, you can rent boats at **Dolphin Marina** (MM 28.5, Little Torch Key; 305-872-2685) and at **Cudjoe Gardens Marina** (MM 21; 305-745-2357).

CANOEING

To explore the shoreline of Biscayne National Park by canoe, contact the **Biscayne Aqua Center** (Convoy Point, east of Homestead; 305-247-2400).

Coral Reef Park Company (MM 102.5, John Pennekamp Coral Reef State Park, Key Largo; 305-451-1621) offers canoes for exploring the park area. In Layton you can rent canoes at **Captain Jerry's Boat Rental** (MM 68.5; 305-664-9393), in Marathon at **Marie's Yacht Harbor Club** (MM 54, 100 Avenue I; 305-743-2442).

SAILING

In the Key Largo area you can rent sailboats from **Coral Reef Park Company** (MM 102.5, John Pennekamp Coral Reef State Park; 305-451-1621). Sailing charters are available from **Sterling Lady Cruises** (MM 100, Key Largo; 305-451-4540), **Witt's End Sailing Charters** (MM 100, Key Largo; 305-451-3354) and **Key Largo Shoal Water Cruises** (MM 96; 305-451-0083).

In Islamorada you can book sailing cruises through **Holiday Isle** (MM 84; 305-664-2321). Go sailing out of Marathon with **Sailmaster Charters** (1000 15th Street, at Boot Key Marina; 305-743-4200) or aboard **Amantha** (MM 48.3, Faro Blanco Resort, Marathon; 305-743-9020).

WINDSURFING

Windsurfers can find boats and lessons at **Windsurfing of the Florida Keys** (MM 104.1, Key Largo; 305-451-3869) and **Coral Reef Park Company** (MM 102.5, John Pennekamp Coral Reef State Park, Key Largo; 305-451-1621). Between Islamorada and Marathon, you can rent windsurfing equipment at **Captain Jerry's Boat Rental** (MM 68.5, Layton; 305-664-9393).

TENNIS

Many Keys resorts provide tennis for their guests. In Islamorada, the public is welcome to play at **The Net** (MM 81; 305-664-4122).

GOLF

At Homestead, visitors are welcome at the **Redland Golf & Country Club** (24451 North Krome Avenue; 305-247-8503).

At Key Colony Beach, near Marathon, the public may play at the nine-hole **Par 3 Golf** (turn off at MM 53.5 and go to 8th Street; 305-289-1533).

HOUSEBOATING

Houseboat vacations in the Keys are available through the **Florida Keys Sailing School** (MM 85.9, Islamorada; 305-664-4009).

BICYCLING

Bikeways parallel Route 1 intermittently down through the Keys.

BIKE RENTALS   You can rent a wide range of bicycles at **Key Largo Bikes** (MM 101.5; 305-451-1910) and at the **KCB Bike Shop** (MM 53, Marathon; 305-289-1670).

Transportation

BY CAR

Route 1 from Miami and the slightly more northerly scenic **Card Sound Road**, which veers off from Route 1 at Florida City, lead to Key Largo, where Route 1 becomes the **Overseas Highway**, continuing through the Keys all the way to Key West.

Note: Mile markers, often called mile posts, can be seen each mile along Route 1 in the Keys. They appear on the right shoulder of the road as small green signs with white numbers, beginning with Mile Marker (MM) 126 just south of Florida City and ending at MM 0 in Key West. When asking for directions in the Keys, your answer will likely refer to a Mile Marker number. We use them throughout the Keys, except for Key West, where street addresses are used.

BY AIR

Many visitors to the Keys choose to fly to Miami (see Chapter Two for more information). However, there are two small airports in the Keys, **Marathon Airport** and **Key West International Airport** (see Chapter Four). Both airports are serviced by Eastern Air Lines/Bar Harbor Express. Marathon airport is also serviced by Airways International and Key West by USAir.

The Airporter (305-247-8874) provides regularly scheduled shuttle service from Miami International Airport to Homestead, Key Largo, Cutler Ridge and Islamorada. **Upper Keys Transportation, Inc.** (305-852-9533) offers limousine service to Miami International Airport on a personally scheduled reservation basis.

BY BUS

Greyhound Bus Lines services Homestead (5 Northeast 3rd Street; 305-247-2040), Tavernier (MM 92.5; 305-852-4666), Islamorada (flagstops along Route 1, 305-852-4666), Marathon (6363 Overseas Highway; 305-743-3488) and Big Pine Key (MM 30.2, 305-872-4022).

CAR RENTALS

Avis Rent A Car (305-743-5428) is located at the Marathon Airport; **Budget Rent A Car** (305-743-7776) and **Hertz Rent A Car** (305-743-6100) will arrange airport pickup.

FOUR

Key West

The Spanish called it *Cayo Hueso,* Island of the Bones. That's what the amazed explorers found when they first landed here—human bones scattered about—but no one ever discovered where they came from. Were they Indian bones? The remains of some grisly massacre? No witness ever came forward to tell the tale. Be that as it may, the word *hueso* was eventually anglicized to "west," and the name "Key West" has stuck through the town's curious and colorful history.

Though not quite in the tropics, Key West is to all appearances a tropical island. Lying low on a shimmering sea, it boasts backyards lush with hibiscus, oleanders, frangipani and kapok and mango trees. Its generous harbors are filled with hybrid fleets of battered fishing craft, glass-bottom boats and handsome yachts. Date and coconut palms rustle like dry paper in the usually gentle and dependable breezes that come in off the sea. Heat pervades, but even in midsummer it's seldom unbearable. Key West is a small town sort of place where narrow streets are lined with picket fences and lovely old frame houses. At the same time, it's a traveler's haven with classy hotels and happy hours. The cul-de-sac of the Overseas Highway, it's unlike any other city in America.

Four miles long from east to west and two miles in width, Key West provides more contrasts than one could dream up for any town, especially one located on a little island over a hundred miles out to sea from mainland Florida. Once the wealthiest city per capita in the country, it was at a later date also the poorest. Men have made fortunes here and have lost them, too, leaving legacies of fine, ornate houses along with quaint, weathered shanties. The military presence has waxed and waned repeatedly as the needs of war have demanded, each time leaving its mark on the architecture and society of the island as well as on the archeology beneath the sands.

115

Tourists have descended in hordes, then gone away, buffeted by the economic status of the nation.

During its trauma-filled history, the city has nearly been destroyed several times—by hurricane, by fire, by economic crises. But Key West has always risen phoenixlike from the ashes of defeats that would have flattened a less determined population. Closer to Havana than to Miami, its residents are descendants of the English, Cuban, Bahamian, African and myriad other folk who have found this tiny place to be an appealing home.

Some of the first residents, after the Indians, were the English Bahamians who came to make their fortunes salvaging the ships that met their doom on the Atlantic reefs. These folks were called "conchs" after the large shells they used for food, decoration and musical instruments. Later came the sponge fishermen who, for a while, provided 90 percent of all sponges sold in the United States. Cigar makers from Cuba numbered as many as 6000, producing millions of hand-rolled cheroots in the late 19th century. Hordes of workers came to continue Henry Flagler's railroad past the Seven Mile Bridge out to Key West about 30 miles away.

Numerous well-known artists and writers, most notably Ernest Hemingway and Tennessee Williams, have found Key West a place of inspiration. The town boasts several Pulitzer Prize winners among its residents. Loafers have discovered Key West to be a comfortable spot for idling away the hospitably temperate days. Gays and others have found a tolerance for their lifestyles. Jazz performers, country-western singers and classical musicians have contributed to the sounds of the little city.

Each group has added color and contrast to the rich island tapestry. Today, Key West is a tourist town, one of the nation's chief travel destinations. Here most visitors have no trouble finding something to their liking. They can find tours and nightlife and souvenir shops. Arts events and festivals and a nightly sunset celebration. Fishing and diving and boat trips to the Gulf Stream and tiny out-islands.

It's easy to stay busy as a tourist here, but it's just as easy to miss some of Key West's most enchanting features. For Key West has held on to many of its contrasts. While you might want to do all the routine visitor activities, you would also be wise to allow yourself enough time to stroll among the old houses, to admire the tropical trees, to taste some *bollitos* at a neighborhood grocery, to fire the imagination with retold tales of pirates and preparation for wars. Plan to tour the cemetery, watch for birds, meet the fishing fleet, explore the fort, talk to folks who live here, and you will begin to get a feel for this most unusual and varied town.

Key West is basically divided into two sections—Old Town, the place where tourists spend most of their time—and the "new town," where residents live and shop and carry out their daily lives.

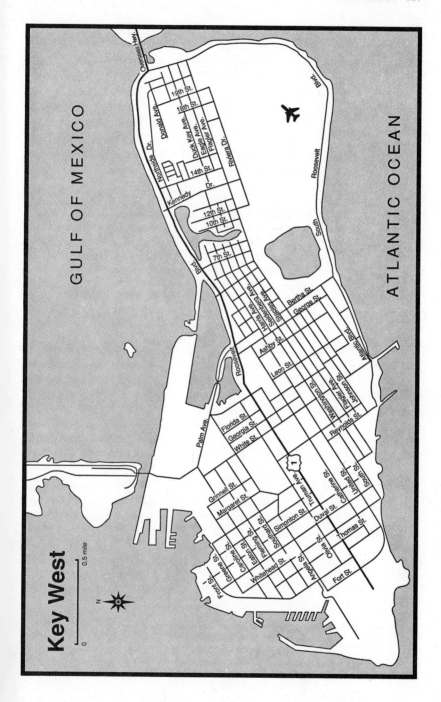

The initial impression of Old Town is usually one of narrow streets, big old houses crowded together, highrise hotels that block the view, too many T-shirt shops and tourists and plenty of confusion. But don't be dismayed. Key West is easy to get to know, and there are all sorts of tours and printed guides and maps to help you. Once you are oriented, you'll have time to enjoy the salt air, to catch a bit of history, to appreciate the brilliant tropical trees whose blossoms gather in a carpet beneath your feet.

Unless you were born here, you will never get to be a genuine "conch," but it will probably not take you long to find plenty to your liking in the great variety of this island city that has never had a frost.

It's easy to get around Key West. The Overseas Highway (Route 1) carries you through the newer section into Old Town via Roosevelt Boulevard. You may go either to the right, along the Gulf of Mexico past the yacht club and marinas, or to the left, along the Atlantic shore. If you take the former route, plan to stop at the **Key West Welcome Center** (3840 North Roosevelt Boulevard; 305-296-4444) for maps and an introduction to the area. This is at about MM 4, but from here on you can stop counting Mile Markers and return to familiar street numbers.

By following Route 1 you will arrive in **Old Town**, the historic and main tourist area of Key West, just about where North Roosevelt Boulevard becomes Truman Avenue. This is a helter-skelter sort of place, with grand old Victorian houses, inviting alleys, junky souvenir shops, rocking and rolling bars, classy hotels, intimate guest houses, crowded marinas, street hawkers and incredible sunsets all tossed together into a colorful, noisy, artsy collage. Thanks to the ghosts of Ernest Hemingway and Tennessee Williams, it has a genuine artistic side, too, continually attracting literary figures and aspiring writers and artists. The gay community is an integral part of Key West's life, too.

Away from Old Town, the remainder of the island includes settled residential areas, predictable shopping and a number of interesting sights that should pull you away from the tourist trappings. Here you are more likely to run into those descendants of old Key West and the Lower Keys who proudly refer to themselves as "conchs." The original settlers were named after the giant shells that were so much a part of their sea-oriented lives.

Although Old Town is small enough for walking, and the whole island for biking, it helps to get oriented on one of several available tours. Besides, you'll pick up some very interesting history of this unique island city. The trackless **Conch Tour Train** (depots near the Welcome Center at 3850 North Roosevelt Boulevard and along Front Street; 305-294-5161) has been orienting visitors for over 30 years with 14-mile island tours. **Old Town Trolley Tour** (leaving every 20 minutes from Mallory Square, the Welcome

Center and most major hotels; 305-296-6688) meanders through the historic old streets.

If you prefer to get oriented on your own, stop at the **Chamber of Commerce** (402 Wall Street; 305-294-2587) and pick up a *Pelican Path* walking tour guide or Solaris Hill's *Walking and Biking Guide to Old Key West.*

You may have to wait in line to have your picture taken at the spot marking the **Southernmost Point** (ocean end of Whitehead Street). "Ninety miles to Cuba," reads the sign beneath the kitschy-looking striped buoy surrounded by folks with cameras.

When you need to cool off and rest your feet, drop in at the basement of the Paradise Shop for a free showing of the 40-minute **Key West Picture Show** (★) (1 Whitehead Street; 305-296-4053). This amusing depiction of island life runs continuously all day. A takeoff on old travelogues and newsreels, it features some notorious local characters and visitors, set against a background of corny music and flashing headlines, such as "The Invasion of the One-Day Tourists."

The factory that was parent to the **Key West Cigar Factory** (3 Pirates Alley off Front Street; 305-294-3470) dates back to the mid-19th century. Though much smaller than the original establishments, this little shop is the place to watch cigars being hand rolled the way they've always been. Cigars are also rolled and sold at **Rodriguez Cigars** (113 Kino Plaza; 305-296-0167).

History buffs will enjoy searching for the gun turret from the **Battleship USS Maine** (near drop boxes at the Post Office, corner of Eaton and Whitehead Streets). Not exactly hidden, but somewhat hard to find, this is a little monument to those who died in the tragic sinking that set off the Spanish-American War.

Take a look at the impressive **Old Stone Methodist Church** (Eaton Street at Duval Street; 305-296-2392), whose two-foot-thick limestone walls were made from solid Key coral rock quarried right beside the sanctuary. Built between 1877 and 1892, the handsome church has a native mahogany ceiling and a teakwood chancel.

The most notable feature of Old Town is the architecture. Many of the beautiful old houses you see were built of wood by ships' carpenters in a blend of styles that came to be known as **conch houses**. Influenced by the varied backgrounds of their owners and the demands of the hurricane-prone climate, the result is an eclectic architectural heritage unique to this island city.

For an introductory sampling of these conch houses, start at the corner of Eaton and William streets, where two **Bahama Houses** stand side by side (703 Eaton Street and 408 William Street). These dwellings are the only ones known to have been shipped in their entirety to Key West from the Bahamas. Built in the mid-1800s by master shipbuilders, they feature unusual beaded siding, mahogany window sashes and broad verandahs.

Next door, the **Samuel Filer House** (724 Eaton Street), built around 1885, is a study in black and white contrasted with an etched cranberry glass transom and double-screen door. Only the front of the **Bartlum/Forgarty House** (718 Eaton Street) was floated over from the Bahamas on a schooner; the mid-19th century dwelling is constructed with wooden pegs.

The large **Richard Peacon House** (712 Eaton Street) was built in the late 1800s by the owner of Key West's largest grocery store. It has distinctive hexagonally shaped verandahs and, some say, a ghost. Calvin Klein purchased it recently for almost a million dollars.

Continue your observations in any direction and you will be enchanted by the charm and variety of so many fine old homes, of which these are only a sample.

The **Audubon House** (Whitehead and Greene streets; 305-294-2116; admission) is an imposing example of early Key West architecture; its restoration inspired a citywide interest in preserving other historic structures. Furnished with fine antiques of the 1830s—the period when John James Audubon visited the Keys—the three-story frame house is held together entirely by wooden pegs and is an excellent example of the shipbuilders' craft. It now serves as a museum housing an extensive collection of works by the famous painter/naturalist.

With delicate double balustrades, beveled glass and fan windows, ornate trim and 26 rooms, the neoclassical **Curry Mansion** (511 Caroline Street; 305-294-5349; admission) presents a three-story display of millionaire life at the turn of the century. Only the Bahama-style hinged shutters are common to other, less opulent homes of early Key West. Today the showcase house is open for tours daily, showing off the luxurious appointments and fine 19th-century furnishings.

Though many famous authors have spent time in Key West, none has left as strong a mark as Ernest Hemingway. He and his wife Pauline bought a beautiful old coral-stone house in which they lived from 1931 until the end of their marriage in 1939. Today, the **Hemingway House** (907 Whitehead Street; 305-296-5811; admission) is a tribute to "Papa's" life and work, for it was here that he created such masterpieces as *A Farewell to Arms* and *For Whom the Bell Tolls*. Tours are given daily, reflecting on Hemingway's works and his rigorous lifestyle. Through the marvelous house and luxuriant grounds roam sleek double-toed cats, said to be descendants of Hemingway's own; they lie irreverently on his works, snooze on his Spanish furniture and stalk the rooms that still reflect the writer's colorful personality.

At the **Key West Aquarium** (1 Whitehead Street; 305-296-2051; admission) you can touch a starfish, watch a shark being fed and see how lobster traps work. Opened in 1932, the aquarium was the first visitors' attraction built in the Keys. Today the small but informative exhibit includes a turtle pool, shark tanks, an ever-growing experimental living coral reef and many other samples of Atlantic and gulf underwater life.

If you've ever wondered how much a gold bar weighs or if rubies still sparkle after centuries on the bottom of the sea, visit **Mel Fisher's Maritime Heritage Society Museum** (200 Greene Street; 305-296-9936; admission). The place literally dazzles with gold chains, jewel-studded crosses and flagons, and great piles of gleaming coins, all treasures gathered by Fisher and his crew of divers from the sunken ships *Atocha* and *Margarita*. You really are allowed to lift the gold bar, though you can't take it with you.

Though nautical archaeologists may frown on treasure seeking today, "wreckers" were once an important part of Keys society, varying from honest salvagers of broken, stranded ships to clever and unscrupulous opportunists. At **The Wrecker's Museum** (322 Duval Street; 305-294-9502; admission) you can learn about this unusual 19th-century profession while also admiring Key West's Oldest House. Built around 1829, this nine-room pine structure houses period antiques, as well as ship models and sea artifacts. Of particular interest is a built-to-scale mid-Victorian conch-style dollhouse complete with a miniature mural of early Key West in its dining room.

Another interesting stop in Key West is the **Hurricane Museum** (201 William Street; 305-294-7522; admission). There is plenty of good information on what conditions make a hurricane and on some notorious storms and famous shipwrecks and lighthouses, as well as advice on what to do when a hurricane is coming your way. There are a few hands-on items; you can even push a button and create a miniature tornado.

Sporting a historically accurate facelift, the **Key West Lighthouse Museum** (938 Whitehead Street; 305-294-0012; admission) is a celebration of the seacoast. Climb the 88 steps to admire the beautiful Fresnel lens and enjoy unsurpassed views of the island and its surrounding seas. The museum houses interesting maritime exhibits including relics and an exquisite model of the U.S. battleship *Maine*, sunk in Havana harbor in 1898.

The city of Key West grows many of its landscaping plants at the **Charles "Sonny" McCoy Indigenous Park** (Atlantic Boulevard at White Street; 305-292-8157), a showplace for trees and plants native to the region. You may wander inside the gates of the park during the daytime and learn to recognize the lignum vitae, silver palm and a number of tropical trees found only in the Keys.

The historic **West Martello Towers** (ocean end of Reynolds Street) are the enchanting home of Key West Garden Club's **Joe Allen Garden Center** (305-294-3210; donations). The remains of the once-upon-a-time fort, with its crumbling brick walls and arches and its massive banyan trees, create a pleasant, restful environment for permanent seed displays, numerous bromeliads and other tropical flora usually confined to greenhouses, and spectacular seasonal displays.

St. Mary Star of the Sea (1010 Windsor Lane; 305-294-1018) is the second oldest Catholic church in Florida. Constructed at the turn of the century of Miami oolite quarried in the Keys, the interesting building features pressed-tin arches and metal columns. Plans are underway for restoration and a museum. On the grounds stands a small **grotto** (★) in honor of the Lady of Lourdes, built many years ago by a nun, who prayed it would provide protection from hurricanes. So far, the grotto seems to have served the purpose she planned, receiving credit from many believers for the absence of any killer storms since the sister's dedicated work was undertaken.

If you take the Conch Tour Train or stroll to the meeting of Margaret and Angela streets, you will see a remarkable **Bottle Wall** built by a Key West artist to keep people (and cars and fire trucks) from cutting through her yard. For a treat, drop by and meet **Carolyn Gorton Fuller** (★) (just strike the gong at the front door). If you buy her book, an artistic, adult coloring book that captures the spirit of Key West, she will show you her home and her eclectic and delightful works of art.

"I Told You I Was Sick," reads the straightforward message immortalized on a gravestone in the **Key West Cemetery** (Angela Street and Passover Lane; 305-292-8177). Due to the rocky geology of the island, many of the stone-encased caskets rest above ground, often carrying curious and humorous messages such as the one placed by a grieving widow: "At Least I Know Where He's Sleeping Tonight." History abounds in this enchanting and poignant spot, too, as in the special memorial to those who died at the sinking of the U.S. Battleship *Maine* in Havana harbor in 1898. You may stroll the cemetery any time; tours are given on weekends.

From the top of the citadel of the **East Martello Museum** (3501 South Roosevelt Boulevard; 305-296-3913; admission) you can get a magnificent view of the island and the Atlantic, just as the builders of this 1862 Civil War brick fortress planned. Today the historic structure houses a large collection of Key West artifacts and serves as both a museum of Key West history and a gallery displaying the work of Keys artists. The fort's tower alone, with vaulted ceilings and spiral staircase, is worth a visit.

Recently rediscovered and unearthed from the sands, the **Fort Zachary Taylor State Historic Site** (★) (western point of island, off Southard Street; 305-292-6713; admission) is a treasure trove of Civil War weaponry and memorabilia. The excavations have revealed beautiful mid-19th-century arched brickwork, parade grounds and the largest collection of Civil War cannons in the United States.

Though Key West may seem all travelers and trolleys, there are several natural spots where the flavor of the real Keys remains. One is the **Thomas**

Riggs Wildlife Refuge (★) (South Roosevelt Boulevard, west of the airport; 305-294-2116). Behind a green chainlink fence stands an observation platform offering a view of the island's salt pond, where heron, ibis, gallinule and other resident and migratory birds gather. Phone the refuge number if the gate is locked.

The Garden Club of Key West owns a small but nicely laid-out and well-marked **Botanical Garden** (★) (Junior College Road and Aguro Circle) where you can get acquainted with some of the trees and other flora that grow in this distinctive region.

The glass-bottom sightseeing boat **Fireball** (north end of Duval Street; 305-296-6293; admission) and the glass-bottom boat of the **Coral Princess Fleet** (700 Front Street; 305-296-3287; admission) make regular runs to the coral reef in the Atlantic, as well as taking visitors on late afternoon sunset cruises.

KEY WEST HOTELS

As you might expect, in Key West you can find countless accommodations from bare-basics motels to outrageously expensive resorts. Especially enticing are the varied guest houses, many of them remodeled Victorian homes from earlier Key West times. A few of the guest houses cater to gays only, and it's okay to inquire. If you want help finding a place to stay, contact the **Key West Reservation Service** (628 Fleming Street; 305-294-7713).

Unless you're up for sleeping on a seawall or pier, you can't spend a night any closer to Cuba than in the nicely renovated, carpeted rooms at **Southernmost Motel in the USA** (1319 Duval Street; 305-296-6577)—it really is what it says. Accommodations are ordinary but gleaming, and the large motel has pseudo-gingerbread trim, two heated pools and a tropical deck with a Tiki bar, all contributing to its being a nice deluxe lodging handy to Key West tourist sights.

Quietly dominating the edge of Old Town, the soft pink, metal-roofed **Hyatt Key West** (601 Front Street; 305-296-9900) is a maze of well-lit stairs and balconies from which you can observe Key West's famous sunsets without the folderol of Mallory Square. The cool pastel decor suits the location beside a tiny private beach and marina. A pool, jacuzzi, exercise room, fine restaurants and indoor/outdoor lounge make this one of the choicest ultra-deluxe lodgings, and one of the most convenient for Key West sightseeing.

Don't let the "Holiday Inn" sign mislead you. **La Concha** (430 Duval Street; 305-296-2991) is unlike any chain hostelry you've experienced. This is a downtown Key West landmark seven-story hotel with a wonderful old-fashioned feel. Holiday Inn was smart not to clone it but to keep its dark woodwork and marble floors and furnish it with appropriate 1920s wicker and wood and hazy old seaside pictures. Walking down the hall and into one of the rooms is like stepping into grandmother's attic trunk. The pool and sundeck, rooftop lounge, restaurants and sidewalk saloon, however, are appropriate toasts to modernity. Deluxe and ultra-deluxe.

La Terraza de Martí (1125 Duval Street; 305-294-8435), popularly known as La-Te-Da, was named for José Martí, who in 1890 campaigned from the front balcony for funds to support the Cuban revolution. Today the original old hotel has grown into a sprawling, helter-skelter maze of rooms and suites tucked among a clutter of porches and balconies and tropical plants. The general effect is borderline art deco, the spirit eclectic—a late-night tropical bar contrasts with the famous Sunday afternoon tea dances. There is a pretty pool and two restaurants, and some of the rooms sport double jacuzzis. Deluxe to ultra-deluxe.

Built in 1890 and sporting a handsome metal-roofed turret on one corner, **The Artist House** (534 Eaton Street; 305-296-3977) is one of many "conch" houses turned hostelry. For deluxe rates, guests may have one of five rooms with private bath, refrigerator and antique or period reproduction furnishings including four-poster or genuine brass beds. The jacuzzi resides in a lush garden among tropical plantings; breakfasts are continental. Rich period wallpapers and superb restoration make this an elegant lodging.

A restored Victorian conch house, **La Mer Hotel** (506 South Street; 305-296-5611) sports contemporary furnishings and definite flair, with tropical plants, oceanview balconies and porches. An elegant complimentary high tea is served during the winter months. Ultra-deluxe.

After a major renovation of this 1880s-era classic revival building, the **Marquesa Hotel** (600 Fleming Street; 305-292-1919) has landed securely on the National Register of Historic Places. Each of the 15 rooms is luxurious and formal, with antique appointments, pastel walls, gleaming white woodwork and distinctive fabrics. Every corner is a masterpiece of workmanship. The property includes a fine restaurant and a sparkling pool. Ultra-deluxe.

Set amid jacaranda, fishtail palm and tamarind and next to an old private tropical garden, **Eaton Lodge** (511 Eaton Street; 305-294-3800) is a fine specimen of Victorian-home-turned-guest-lodge. Authentically restored with polished floors, high ceilings and period furnishings, every room has a private bath and a verandah or patio facing onto the lush gardens. A continental breakfast is included in the deluxe to ultra-deluxe price tag.

For a moderate rate, you can stay at **Eden House** (1015 Fleming Street; 305-296-6868) and share a bath, or you can go deluxe and have your privacy. A friendly wicker-furnished lobby invites socializing. The rooms in this 1920s-era guest house are functional and simple, but a lovely second-floor deck sits among the treetops and a nice pool lies below. Eden House offers newer efficiencies, too, some with french doors leading onto pleasant screened porches.

The **Curry Mansion Inn** (511 Caroline Street; 305-294-5349) provides 15 rooms with private baths. Most are in the beautiful backyard annex that surrounds the pretty deck and outdoor jacuzzi, though several are in the fine old historic mansion itself. Furnishings are mostly top-of-the-line wicker, and every bed is covered with a handmade quilt. Rooms in the annex are all pastel and white, creating a cool, fresh feel even on the hottest summer day. Deluxe to ultra-deluxe rates include complimentary happy hour, membership in a nearby beach club and a continental breakfast with various fresh-baked breads.

If you remember old-fashioned tourist courts, then you can indulge in a bit of nostalgia at **Key Lime Village** (727 Truman Avenue; 305-294-6222), a collection of 1920s and 1930s cottages surrounding an 1854 home. The accommodations are tiny but functional, including efficiency apartments and motel-type rooms with shared baths. There are no televisions or phones, but it's all very peaceful. Moderate.

A member of the international Youth Hostel Association, the **Key West Hostel** (★) (718 South Street; 305-296-5719) has budget-priced dorm rooms for males, females and marrieds. All ages are welcome, but nonmembers must have a valid ID. There are full kitchen facilities and lockers and bicycles to rent.

Even if you don't choose to stay at **Casa Marina** (Reynolds Street on the ocean; 305-296-3535), you should drop in and indulge in the Sunday brunch or at least explore the lobby of this 1921 historic landmark, created as the final resort along Henry Flagler's railroad. This handsome Spanish-style hotel radiates historic elegance. The pine floors gleam like glass. The french doors leading to a spacious loggia, and the restaurant's restored mahogany coffered ceiling pay tribute to Flagler's dreams for the Keys. A beachfront pavilion, lighted tennis courts, pool and water sports center add modern luxury. Ultra-deluxe.

If you prefer being away from the Old Town crowds and close to a great expanse of Atlantic beachfront, the **Key Wester** (3675 South Roosevelt Boulevard; 305-296-5671) is a perfect location. There's a great seawall for strolling just across the street, and the airport, a public beach and two excellent restaurants are close by. Rooms and efficiencies are run-of-the-mill but neat and clean; individual villas have little screened porches looking out onto the spacious grounds. The Olympic-sized pool with diving board is said to be the only one of its kind in the Keys, and there are tennis courts, sauna, bicycles and an outdoor bar. Moderate, with terrific off-season discounts.

KEY WEST RESTAURANTS

The big sunken bar and the dark pub-like atmosphere make the **Full Moon Saloon** (1202 Simonton Street; 305-294-9090) a friendly and slightly uproarious eating and drinking place. You can get a full meal here until at least 3 a.m. Most of the fare is seafood, with emphasis on local specialties such as conch prepared in a variety of fashions and freshly smoked fish. Budget to moderate.

The **Pigeon House Patio** (301 Whitehead Street; 305-296-9600) does have two lovely candlelit indoor dining areas, including one with handpainted ceiling borders, but the choicest spot is outside among the jungly vines and dangling banyan tree roots. The restaurant is named for the carrier pigeons that were cooped here when not carrying messages between the United States and Cuba during World War II. Pan American Airlines was born in the building, hence the chief entrée is Pan Am Fettucine, a shrimp, ham and vegetable mélange rich with brandy cream sauce. Deluxe.

The sign above the **Crab Shack** (908 Caroline Street; 305-294-9658) promises "free crab tomorrow," but don't be discouraged if tomorrow never comes; the "all you can eat" spicy steamed shrimp is no hoax, if you dine between 5 and 9:30 p.m. Most of the meals here are moderately priced, and the crab selections are especially impressive for they include imports from Maryland and Alaska as well as the local side-crawlers. You can eat inside or out in dining areas that are rustic and functional. There's a good assortment of combination dinners that include both seafood and meat.

The Buttery (1208 Simonton Street; 305-294-0717) keeps getting rave reviews from reviewers who enjoy raving, and who seem to also enjoy good food. White cloths, crystal, punched-tin lamps and a blue-and-white emphasis make this deluxe restaurant very attractive. Sit beneath the soaring skylight or under low ceilings to enjoy the elegant ways the Buttery prepares seafood, fowl and meats, especially veal, which the chef treats differently every night. Vegetarian pasta, yellowtail baked with bananas and walnuts, and an unusual ceviche made from shrimp, scallops and (naturally) conch are some of the interesting menu items.

With candlelight, pink linens and a choice of indoor or poolside dining, the **La-Te-Da** (1125 Duval Street; 305-294-8435) restaurant in La Terraza de Martí hotel offers a deluxe to ultra-deluxe menu that includes a four-course prix fixe dinner and some interesting treatments of local seafood. Or try the *poulet rôti croûte d'ail*, which is roasted chicken in a garlic crust with pineapple chutney, or the sautéed calf's liver with red onion marmalade and diced pancetta.

Up among the treetops at La Terraza de Martí hotel is the **Crystal Café** (1125 Duval Street; 305-294-8435), a very art deco supper club with a classy black-and-white tile-and-chrome bar and piano music. Open far into the night, the café offers moderate to deluxe nightly specials and a small menu of pastas, meats and seafoods, including various treatments of Florida lobster. The "antipasto party" special is a gourmet tasting feast and a meal in itself.

For a hearty budget meal, **El Loro Verde** (404 Southard Street; 305-296-7298), basically a small, cheerful, formica-boothed restaurant, offers traditional Mexican fare with a few Caribbean touches and some slightly different seafood entrées such as scallop ceviche. There is a wide variety of domestic and imported beers to accompany the chips and hot and mild salsas; chalkboard entrées, such as fish Barbados with mutton peppers, vary from day to day.

Louie's Back Yard (700 Wadell Street; 305-294-1061) resides in a beautifully restored classical revival conch house with a tin roof, spacious verandahs and airy 12-foot-high rooms with polished floors and fine art. Best of all, though, is the view of the sea that you can enjoy from the deck or through the generous windows. Louie's ultra-deluxe menu earns top rankings from food critics and includes such creative fare as smoked barbecue duck salad with Oriental noodles and Szechuan dressing.

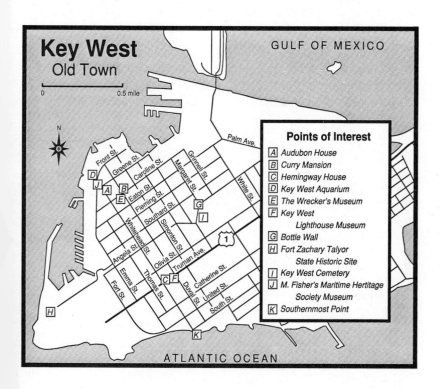

Key West
Old Town

0   0.5 mile

N

GULF OF MEXICO

Palm Ave.

Points of Interest

A Audubon House
B Curry Mansion
C Hemingway House
D Key West Aquarium
E The Wrecker's Museum
F Key West
    Lighthouse Museum
G Bottle Wall
H Fort Zachary Talyor
    State Historic Site
I Key West Cemetery
J M. Fisher's Maritime Hertitage
    Society Museum
K Southernmost Point

Front St.
Greene St.
Caroline St.
Grinnell St.
Margaret St.
White St.
Eaton St.
Fleming St.
Whitehead St.
Southard St.
Simonton St.
Angela St.
Olivia St.
Truman Ave.
Emma St.
Thomas St.
Duval St.
Catherine St.
United St.
South St.
Fort St.

ATLANTIC OCEAN

Located just out of reach of the ocean tides of South Beach, **The Eatery** (1405 Duval Street; 305-294-2727) keeps the crowds coming all day long. It is the perfect answer for both the very hungry and the very undecided, because every meal is an all-you-can-eat buffet. Dinner is moderately priced, meaning you can indulge in all the steamed shrimp you can hold without breaking the bank. And there's always conch chowder, conch fritters, seasonal fish as well as options such as ribs, chicken and pork for land-food-lovers. Lots of locals come here to dine beside the sea.

For such succulent Cuban dishes as black beans and yellow rice, fried plantains, *picadillo* and those wonderful famous sandwiches of thick slices of meat and cheese on crusty Cuban bread, go to **La Lechonera** (3100 Flagler Avenue; 305-296-7881). Forget your diet; the theme here is pigs. Poster porkers line the walls, imparting such wisdom as, "a moment on the lips, forever on the hips" and "fat is beautiful." Budget to moderate.

The first thing you notice at **Martha's** (3591 South Roosevelt Boulevard; 305-294-3466) is the lovely and clever decor. Slender vertical lighted fish tanks seem magically suspended in midair. Each dining level is raised slightly above the one in front of it, affording everyone a view of the Atlantic that lies beyond the broad glass expanse. In this land of the sea and its harvests, however, Martha's is noted for it prime rib and other beef dishes, though there are plenty of seafood entrées. Another unusual twist is lobster stuffed with chicken. There's an impressive wine list and piano music every night. Deluxe.

For a filling and tasty budget meal, try **El Siboney** (★) (900 Catherine Street; 305-296-4184), a Cuban restaurant where they serve generous portions of *ropa vieja* (it means "old clothes," but it's really a beef dish), *bistec de wasa* (jewfish steak), stuffed shrimp and crab and some fine pork dishes—all with black beans and rice. Other side dishes include *plátanos* and *casava*, a sometimes tasteless starchy yucca dish, but here well seasoned and worth a try because it's good for you. White lace cloths add a touch of class to this plain family place.

To feed a hungry family, drive over to Stock Island and enjoy traditional seafood, steaks, chicken or barbecue at the **Hickory House** (★) (5948 Maloney Avenue; 305-294-1788). This long-established, off-the-beaten-path eatery resides in an old, lodge-style house surrounded by a white fence and palm trees. Dependable food and all-you-can-eat specials such as baby-back ribs and chicken make this worth the short drive. Moderate.

The Rusty Anchor (★) (5th Avenue off 5th Street across from the dog track, Stock Island; 305-294-5369) is run by a local family who have turned a one-time leaky-floored shrimpers' bar into a favored eating spot for locals from Key West and elsewhere. Charter boat captains send their customers here because, as one said, "It's just the best," a good example of the word-of-mouth publicity that keeps folks coming. The location is unlikely, proving that the reputation of good seafood, well-prepared conch fritters and, surprisingly, barbecued baby-back ribs, are all it takes to make an open-air eatery a success.

KEY WEST SHOPPING

Key West is the place to spend your money. The Old Town streets in the waterfront area are a mass of shops and boutiques offering everything from imported flamingos to artful fabrics. Visitors do most of their shopping in the dozens of glitzy and funky shops in Old Town; practical shopping is available in several centers in the newer areas.

Not quite all the sponge fishermen are gone from Key West, as explained on a continuous video at the **Sponge Market** (1 Whitehead Street; 305-294-2555). Elderly sponger C. B. McHugh demonstrates the harvesting and treating of sponges and tells their history on the film; the store has bins of these marvelous nonpolyfoam wonders.

Located in a historic old one-time waterfront grocery, the **Key West Art Center** (301 Front Street; 305-294-1241) is a cooperative for local artists. Works for sale include paintings and drawings of seascapes, sunsets and Key West street scenes, as well as sculpture and other art.

Brightly colored silkscreened fabrics and designer clothing are for sale at **Key West Hand Print Fabrics** (201 Simonton Street; 305-294-9535). You can watch the process of this local industry in the next-door printing factory.

Cavanaugh's (520 Front Street; 305-296-3343) has a wide variety of imported items for amazingly reasonable prices. This big store features furnishings and gifts from around the world, including Oaxacan pottery, Oriental accessories, Latin American treasures and a boundless supply of baskets. There is a selection of sporty clothing, but the main attractions here are the imports.

If you don't plan to go deep-sea treasure hunting yourself, you can arrange to buy an authentic piece of booty at **Mel Fisher's Treasure Exhibit and Sales** (200 Greene Street; 305-296-6533).

Though he's usually on the road performing and recording, Jimmy Buffet and his eclectic blend of Caribbean and cowboy music have become a trademark of Key West, where the singer got his start. Now Buffet fans can pop into his local **Margaritaville Store** (500 Duval Street; 305-296-3070) for all kinds of memorabilia from tapes to T-shirts. A portion of the profits from the shop and its monthly newsletter/catalog, *Coconut Telegraph*, go to the "Save the Manatee Fund," one of Buffet's numerous environmental projects.

For exotic kites, colorful windsocks and just about any toy that flies, visit **Heavenly Body Kites** (409 Greene Street; 305-296-2535).

If **Kino Sandals** (424 Greene Street; 305-294-9535) doesn't have a perfect pair of their uncomplicated footwear to fit you, they can make you some on the spot. They've been making sandals for men, women and children for almost as long as anyone can remember.

At the **Key West Fragrance & Cosmetic Factory** (540 Greene Street; 305-294-5592) you can see them make cosmetics from aloe vera, try samples and purchase the popular suntan, skincare and hair products for men and women. **Key West Aloe** (524 Front Street; 305-294-5592) also carries all the aloe vera cosmetics as well as many other boutique items.

If the **Sea Store** (★) (614 Greene Street; 305-294-3438) isn't open when you go by, it's probably because the owners are out dealing with important ecological matters, which makes them expert advisors on local wildlife and natural habitats. If it is closed, come back later and browse among shipwreck treasures such as old bottles, barnacle-encrusted cannonballs, ballast stones and pieces-of-eight from galleons. The store also carries some works by local artists, including fine handcrafted tropic wood and driftwood pieces designed by the owner.

Dansk Factory Outlet (400 Duval Street; 305-294-0151) carries a wide collection of dinnerware, teakwood serving pieces, flatware, glassware, cookware and gifts, including many discontinued patterns and factory seconds.

Fast Buck Freddie's (500 Duval Street; 305-294-2007) is a wonderful hodgepodge of a department store left over from the days before malls. Browse through racks of trendy tropical clothing, funny posters, fine candies, fancy fabrics, home furnishings and all sorts of gift items.

The appropriately beautiful and aloof "Madame" will greet you at **The Cat House** (411 Greene Street; 305-294-4779), a full-service gift shop for all cats (such as "Madame") and cat lovers. You'll find T-shirts, cards, toys and other purr-fect gifts.

For books on sunken treasure, seafaring tales, marine archaeology and naval history, stop in at **Seafarers Nautique Studio/Gallery** (2 Charles Street; 305-292-1301), where you will also find shipwreck coins, marine art, nautical jewelry and, of course, T-shirts.

Haitian Art Co. (600 Frances Street; 305-296-8932) imports sculptures, carvings, papier-mâché and brilliantly colored paintings in handcrafted frames by Haitian artists.

The **Key West Island Bookstore** (513 Fleming Street; 305-294-2904) carries a large collection of literature about Key West and books by authors who have lived here. They also have new, used and rare volumes.

Those concerned with the environment will be interested in the posters, T-shirts and other ecology-oriented souvenirs at **Greenpeace Gift Store** (612 Duval Street; 305-296-4442), where all proceeds go to campaigns such as saving whales, turtles and dolphins.

There's a real "hammock expert" to help you at **Hats & Hammocks** (605 Whitehead Street; 305-294-2627), which carries a huge selection of these relaxing items as well as imported Mexican and Guatemalan folk art.

Because it's away from the bustling commercial area, you might miss **Whitehead Street Pottery (★)** (1011 Whitehead Street; 305-294-5067), located in what was once a Cuban grocery. Every piece here is one-of-a-kind, including many beautiful and durable copper-red and raku art pieces glazed with metallic oxides.

It's hard to know whether **Five Brothers Grocery (★)** (930 Southard Street; 305-296-5205) should be classified as a shop or a restaurant, but I'll choose the former because there are no chairs or tables, just some cramped shelves of basic groceries and some favorite items for local Spanish cooking. The main reason for stopping here, though, is the counter food; locals maintain the Cuban sandwiches and *bollitos* are the best anywhere. You can also take out espresso, *café con leche, papa rellena* and a can of papaya for dessert. This is not a tourist place but a tiny neighborhood grocery. In fact, a sign warns, "This isn't Burger King. You do it My Way!"

KEY WEST NIGHTLIFE

If you wondered where the nighttime action was as you traveled down the Keys, you'll discover it's almost all here in Key West. Entertainment begins long before sunset and goes on far into the early morning hours. A number of nightclubs seem to spill right out through their open windows and doors and onto the street.

Sunset in Key West is an *event*, so don't miss it. Join the crowds of visitors, performers and hawkers of wares who gather each late afternoon at **Mallory Square** (northwest end of Duval Street). To bagpipes and drums and cheers from the crowd, the sun dependably disappears into the sea every night (unless it's overcast, which is rare), providing Key West's most spectacular and least costly evening's entertainment.

You should at least stick your head into **Sloppy Joe's** (201 Duval Street; 305-294-8585) because it has hooked onto the Papa Hemingway legend in as many ways as it can. Papa and Sloppy Joe were drinking buddies, apparently, and it's said that some of the tales that showed up in literature were founded on stories they shared in the backroom here. Just follow your ears and you'll find it most anytime of the day or night; there's live rock, rhythm-and-blues and other varied entertainment until 2 a.m.

Captain Tony's Saloon (428 Greene Street; 305-294-1838), "where everybody is a star," is said to be the location of the *real* Sloppy Joe's, and it just may be true. Anyway, the real star here is Captain Tony, a wiry white-haired codger who has polished his role as local character until it shines. Rowdy and fun, with all sorts of live performers, it's a Key West institution.

Two Friends Patio Restaurant (512 Front Street; 305-296-9212) features live Dixieland jazz, calypso and blues every night in its big, popular open-air lounge, and the festivities sometimes spill out onto the street. There is a restaurant attached and a raw bar for late-night eating.

You'll find a bar, rock-and-roll and, of course, plenty of Jimmy Buffet music at the **Margaritaville Café** (500 Duval Street; 305-292-1435), where Jimmy, no longer "wastin' away," makes occasional impromptu appearances.

For live music till 2 a.m., drop in at **Casa Marina's Calabash Lounge** (Reynolds Street on the ocean; 305-296-3535), where you can dance to Top-40 tunes in a glamorous, brass-and-glass, 150-seat nightclub surrounded by history.

On the sunset deck of second-story **Havana Docks Bar** (Pier House, 1 Duval Street; 305-294-9541) you can get an eyeful of the Gulf and an earful of the Top-40 band entertaining the crowd. Dancing and revelry goes on late into the night. Cover for indoor lounge only.

There's nightly entertainment at the **Turtle Kraal Bar** (2 Land's End Village, end of Margaret Street; 305-294-2640), once a turtle cannery and now an old-style Key West eating and drinking spot. You can see turtles and other sea creatures here while you relax and have a drink.

The Top (430 Duval Street; 305-296-2991) has the best view of any night spot in Key West, from the top of the 1925 La Concha hotel. There's dancing and live "island" music nightly, following, of course, the sunsets.

The arts are alive in Key West, too. A variety of popular and classical concerts, plays and dance programs are presented at the **Tennessee Williams Fine Arts Center** (5901 Junior College Road; 305-294-6232).

The **Waterfront Playhouse** (Mallory Square; 305-294-5015) offers an assortment of plays, films, reviews and musical comedies throughout the winter and spring. For an evening of dinner and theater, check the schedule of **Jan McArts Cabaret Theatre** (410 Wall Street; 305-296-2120). **The Red Barn Theatre** (319 Duval Street; 305-296-9911) is a resident company presenting several productions during the winter season.

A number of artistic events take place as part of various long-running festivals during the high season, too. Contact **Florida Keys Arts Explo** (305-296-5000, ext. 357), **Old Island Days** (305-294-9501) and **Festival of the Continents** (305-296-5882) to see what's happening where during your stay.

Dog racing takes off six nights a week at **Berensons' Key West Greyhound Track** (Stock Island; 305-294-9517).

KEY WEST BEACHES AND PARKS

It's a surprise to many visitors that Key West has very few beaches, and those it does have are far from sensational. On the south side of the island, along the Atlantic Ocean, you can dip into the water or lie in the sun at one of several narrow public beaches that tend to get very crowded.

Smathers Beach—A long narrow strip of hard sand, this spot's most attractive feature is the wonderfully clear water that allows even uninitiated snorkelers to engage in eye-to-eye contact with colorful sea creatures. A city-owned beach, Smathers is where locals lie in the sun in the daytime and take walks at night.

Facilities: Restrooms, water-sport rentals. *Swimming:* Nice water but rocky bottom.

Getting there: Off Atlantic Boulevard west of the airport.

Higgs Beach—This county beach features a fishing pier from which swimmers and snorkelers have easy access to the inviting Atlantic. Although the sandy area is unassuming, the safe shallows and number of nearby recreational facilities make it a popular spot for families.

Facilities: Picnic areas, restrooms, bathhouse, playground, tennis courts, water-sport rentals. *Swimming:* Permitted.

Getting there: Located along Atlantic Boulevard between White Street and Reynolds Road.

Fort Zachary Taylor State Historic Site—Though the chief attraction here is the excavated and restored fort, the park also contains one of the nicest little beaches, especially for sunset-viewing and boat-watching, in the area. A grove of trees provides some rare seaside shade.

Facilities: Picnic areas, restrooms; information, 305-292-6713. *Swimming:* Good, but watch for drop-offs.

Getting there: Located off the western end of Southard Street.

The Sporting Life

SPORTFISHING

From Key West you can go fishing for a few hours in the Atlantic or for several days on the Tortuga Banks; there are dozens of craft and fleets to choose from, such as **Sea-Faris** (Land's End Marina, end of Margaret Street; 305-294-7009), **Sea Breeze Charters** (25 Arbutus Drive; 305-294-6027) and **MV Florida Fish Finders** (1 Front Street on Stock Island; 305-296-0111).

(Text continued on page 136.)

Fort Jefferson

Like a scattering of tiny emerald beads, a cluster of coral reef islands dot the Gulf of Mexico 68 miles west of Key West. Ponce de León named them "Tortugas" for the turtles he found there; sailors called them "Dry" because they hold no fresh water. But the Dry Tortugas do hold a national monument, centered around a magnificent 19th-century fort.

To see **Fort Jefferson** (for information, contact the U.S. Coast Guard in Key West; 305-247-6211) from the air, surrounded by azure sea, walled moat and white sand, is like conjuring up a fairy tale, enriched with popular legends of pirate treasure. Walking through the open sally port and arched hallways, one steps into a vast area whose silence is broken only by seagull cries and the calls of migratory birds.

Fort Jefferson, from its perch on Garden Key, appears much as it did in its brief 19th-century heyday. German and Irish craftsmen, with the assistance of slaves, created the spectacular brick-and stonework from millions of bricks brought by sailing ships from Pensacola and Virginia, and granite and slate brought from New England. The eight-foot-thick walls stand 50 feet high and feature handsome arches and wide views of sea approaches. Fort Jefferson's half-mile hexagonal perimeter made it the largest link in the chain of coastal fortifications built from Maine to Texas in the first half of the 19th century. It encompasses almost all the land of its tiny key, creating the illusion that it floats on the glistening tropical sea.

Though at first glance the fort seems complete, it was never actually finished. Begun in 1846, work continued for 30 years, but Fort Jefferson's importance came to an end with the invention of the rifled cannon. When federal troops occupied the fort throughout the Civil War, they discovered its foundations were not built on solid coral reef as was originally thought, but on sand and coral boulders. The walls began to show cracks as foundations settled with the shifting of the sea floor.

Fort Jefferson's most inglorious claim to fame came in 1865. To this lonely and inescapable reef were sent the "Lincoln Conspirators," four men convicted of complicity in the assassination of President Abraham Lincoln. Most noted of these was Dr. Samuel Mudd, the physician who had innocently set the broken leg of John Wilkes Booth following the shooting of the president. Sentenced to life imprisonment at Fort Jefferson, Mudd was eventually pardoned following his gallant efforts at treating the almost 300 garrisoned men who were struck with yellow fever at the fort during the 1867 epidemic. Today visitors can explore Mudd's cell and envision the bleakness of his fate.

The Army formally abandoned Fort Jefferson in 1874, following more yellow fever and a serious hurricane; it never saw military action. And many military men may have felt grateful, for duty at Fort Jefferson, where water was scarce, mosquitoes thick and hurricane winds ferocious, was not coveted. But fortunately for historians and travelers, President Franklin D. Roosevelt proclaimed Fort Jefferson a national monument in 1935, thus preserving its unique heritage and its spectacular architecture.

To visit Fort Jefferson, you must go by chartered seaplane with **Key West Seaplane Service** (5603 West Junior College Road, Key West; 305-294-6978) or by boat. The plane trip rewards visitors with breathtaking views of the shallow waters, shipwrecks and coral reefs off the tip of the state.

You can spread a picnic, pitch a tent in the shade of tropical trees or sunbathe on the tiny, pristine beach, but you must bring everything with you, for only restrooms are available on the island. An excellent self-guiding tour, introduced by an explanatory slide show, orients visitors to the wonderful wild fort that you may roam to your heart's content. Snorkelers need only wade out waist-deep from the little beach to behold the colorful array of marine creatures that dart among the patches of living coral in the crystal-clear Gulf water.

SKINDIVING

You can scuba or snorkel by making arrangements with **Reef Raiders Dive Shop** (109 Duval Street; 305-294-3635), **Key West Pro Dive Shop** (1605 North Roosevelt Boulevard; 305-296-3823) and **Seasports Dive Center** (101 Margaret Street; 305-294-6224), among many.

BOATING

Boat rentals are abundant in Key West, in places such as **Key West Boat Rental** (617 Front Street; 305-294-2628) and **Club Nautico** (717-C Eisenhower Drive; 305-294-2225).

SAILING

For sailing trips with crews out of Key West, try **Mariposa Charters** (Land's End Marina, north end of Margaret Street; 305-294-1525) or **Miss Texas** (Hyatt Marina, Simonton and Front streets; 305-296-0649). For catamaran cruises, contact **Key West Catamarans** (328 Simonton Street; 305-294-5687).

WINDSURFING

Windsurfers, jet skis and other water-sport craft are available from entrepreneurs who set up shop alongside Smathers and Higgs beaches. For information and options, try **Watersports on the Atlantic** (305-294-2696) or **Sunset Watersports** (305-296-2554).

GOLF

On Stock Island, **The Key West Resort** (305-294-5232) has an 18-hole course with public tee-times.

TENNIS

Some of the resorts and country clubs provide courts for their guests and allow the public to play for a fee. In Key West you can play for no charge at **Bayview Park** (1310 Truman Avenue; 305-294-1346). There are also public courts at **Higgs County Beach** (Atlantic Boulevard between White Street and Reynolds Road; 305-294-2305).

BICYCLING

Bicycling is a good way to explore Key West. Residents and visitors alike can be seen pedaling around on "conch cruisers," which seem to be any old bikes whose handlebars have been replaced with high-handled affairs that look just right in Key West.

BIKE RENTALS   Bikes can be rented from **The Bicycle Center** (523 Truman Avenue; 305-294-4556), **Bubba's Bike Rental** (705 Duval Street; 305-294-2618) and **Holiday Rental** (512 Greene Street; 305-296-1745).

Transportation

BY CAR

Route 1, the **Overseas Highway**, leads directly over the bridge from neighboring Stock Island into Key West. You can reach Old Town by following Roosevelt Boulevard either to the right or left, along the Gulf of Mexico or the Atlantic Ocean. Once in Old Town, auto driving is difficult, particularly in the high season. Sightseeing is best done on foot or bicycle or via the tour train or trolley (see Key West sightseeing in this chapter).

BY AIR

Many visitors to Key West choose to fly to Miami (see Chapter Two for more information). However, you can also fly into the small **Key West International Airport**, which is serviced by Delta/Comair, Eastern Air Lines/Bar Harbor Express and USAir.

BY BUS

Greyhound Bus Lines services Key West (615½ Duval Street; 305-296-9072).

CAR RENTALS

See Chapter Two for information on car rentals at the Miami airport.

Rental agencies located at the Key West airport include **Avis Rent A Car** (305-296-8744) and **Dollar Rent A Car** (305-296-9921). Pickup at the airport can be arranged through **Alamo Rent A Car** (305-294-6675), **Budget Rent A Car** (305-294-8868), **Hertz Rent A Car** (305-294-1039) and **Thrifty Rent A Car** (305-296-6514).

PUBLIC TRANSPORTATION

The **City of Key West Port and Transit Authority** (305-292-8165) operates buses that run the entire length and partial width of the island. Curiously, the route does not include the airport.

TAXIS

Taxicabs that serve the Key West airport include **A Better Cab Company** (305-294-4444) and **AAA Sun Cab Company** (305-296-7777).

Index

Note: Hotel and restaurant names are not indexed; names of beaches, parks, and major sightseeing spots are.

About the Author

Candace Leslie is a co-author of Ulysses Press' *Hidden Florida* and of *Weekend Escapes, Southeast Texas,* published by Rand McNally. Her work has appeared in *Readers' Digest, Amtrak Express, Diversion,* the *Boston Herald, Texas Highways* and other publications. A member of the Society of American Travel Writers, Candace is also Travel Editor of *Insite Magazine.* She was raised in Florida, a state she has "rediscovered" and writes about often.

About the Illustrator

Norman Nicholson, a graduate of the Art Center College of Design in Los Angeles, has successfully combined a career in illustration and painting. His artwork has appeared in national ads, book and magazine illustrations and posters. His paintings have hung in the Smithsonian, the White House and the California State Capitol Building. He currently teaches painting at the Academy of Art in San Francisco.

Also Available From Ulysses Press

CALIFORNIA: THE ULTIMATE GUIDEBOOK
Definitive. From the Pacific to the desert to the Sierra Nevada, it captures the best of the Golden State. 504 pages. $13.95

HIDDEN HAWAII
Award winning guide to the islands. Completely revised and updated. 400 pages. $12.95

HIDDEN MEXICO
Covers the entire 6000-mile Mexican coastline in the most comprehensive fashion ever. 432 pages. $12.95

HIDDEN FLORIDA
A perfect companion for anyone exploring the Sunshine State. 492 pages. $12.95

HIDDEN MIAMI, FORT LAUDERDALE AND PALM BEACH
Focuses on the most popular stretch of coastline in all Florida. 192 pages. $7.95

HIDDEN COAST OF CALIFORNIA
Explores the fabled California coast from Mexico to Oregon. 444 pages. $12.95

HIDDEN SOUTHERN CALIFORNIA
The most complete guidebook to Los Angeles and Southern California in print. 516 pages. $12.95

HIDDEN SAN FRANCISCO AND NORTHERN CALIFORNIA
A major resource for travelers exploring the Bay Area and beyond. 432 pages. $12.95

TO ORDER DIRECT For each book send an additional $2 postage and handling (California residents include 6% sales tax) to Ulysses Press, P.O. Box 4000–H, Berkeley, CA 94704